"*Closing Costs* provides a much-needed resource for churches facing a transitional crossroads. But this isn't just a practical workbook, for Dominic grounds his thinking in the missional imperative of outward discipleship and community engagement in Jesus Christ. It's a must-read for every lay and clergy member who faces an uncertain future—and that is all of us!"

—GRANT HAGIYA, Resident Bishop, California-Pacific and Desert Southwest Annual Conferences, The United Methodist Church

"It's always hard for churches to face uncertainty. The decision-making process can be paralyzing. This book provides practical insight that opens up new opportunities that churches should seriously consider. I recommend Dominic not only as an expert in his field but also as a friend and fellow follower of Jesus."

—JOSH WROTEN, Lead Pastor, Grace Church

"If you're about to embark on a building project or strategic plan, if you're a member or leader of a faith-based organization, if you're searching for a way to integrate the sacred and civil, then you are ready to read *Closing Costs*."

—GLADYS GUENTHER, SHF

"Thousands of churches will need to close or repurpose their buildings in the coming years. Dutra lifts up three options that churches facing closure may want to consider: merging, leasing, or selling their buildings. . . . Dutra calls us to focus primarily on mission and the good of our communities. Church death is not to be feared, for it presents an opportunity to give—and maybe even experience for oneself—new life."

—MARK ELSDON, author of *We Aren't Broke*

"*Closing Costs* offers resurrection hope. Through inspiring real-life examples, a prophet's piercing analysis, and the culled wisdom of decades of experience, Dutra exhorts struggling faith communities to remember their mission . . . to care for the wounded and needy in our world. As you walk the Emmaus road of coming to terms with the impending death of your congregation, he is the companion that you want by your side."

—FRANK ROGERS JR., author of *Compassion in Practice*

"I am delighted that Dutra has put together this very practical resource. This book is the fruition of his long career of helping institutions explore their purpose and mission for the future. *Closing Costs* is a wonderful and timely resource that will benefit churches tremendously during this uncertain time for organized religion."

—KAH-JIN JEFFREY KUAN, President and Professor of Hebrew Bible, Claremont School of Theology

"*Closing Costs* is the book your church needs, no matter its size, location, or denomination. . . . What Dominic offers in *Closing Costs* is an approach that every church should consider. Nothing is lost and everything is gained in connecting with and serving local communities, using our spaces for the glory of God and the care of God's people."

—JOHN HARVEY TAYLOR, Seventh Bishop of Los Angeles, Episcopal Diocese of Los Angeles

"After the Torah, 1–2 Kings, and the Prophets come the books of wisdom. That is the section where I would place Dominic's book on reimagining church real estate. He offers very pragmatic wisdom strongly tied to the discipleship of following Jesus and equally tied to the mission of the church. Dutra uses his gifts and experience well to provide a missional conversation about property that is, above all, healthy and faithful."

—GIL RENDLE, author of *Quietly Courageous*

Closing Costs

Closing Costs

Reimagining Church Real Estate for Missional Purposes

DOMINIC DUTRA

Foreword by Albert Hung

RESOURCE *Publications* • Eugene, Oregon

CLOSING COSTS
Reimagining Church Real Estate for Missional Purposes

Resource Publications
An Imprint of Wipf and Stock Publishers
199 W. 8th Ave., Suite 3
Eugene, OR 97401

www.wipfandstock.com

PAPERBACK ISBN: 978-1-6667-1168-4
HARDCOVER ISBN: 978-1-6667-1169-1
EBOOK ISBN: 978-1-6667-1170-7

VERSION NUMBER 122121

Above all, this book is dedicated to God, who for some unknown reason chose to reveal himself to me when I least deserved it and, in doing so, changed my life forever.

To my wife Lisa, who for over thirty-five years has been the love of my life and my best friend.

And to my beautiful children, Tricia and Gabriel, for the endless joy you bring me every day.

Contents

Foreword by Albert Hung | IX
Acknowledgements | XIII

Introduction | 1
1 To Live Is Christ, To Die Is Gain | 8
2 A Call to Jubilee | 29
3 So That Our Joy May Be Made Complete | 40
4 Parables on Merging | 50
5 With Glad and Sincere Hearts | 62
6 Parables on Leasing | 71
7 Our Light Affliction | 89
8 Parables on Selling | 99
9 Pressing on Toward the Goal | 116
10 Testing Everything, Holding Fast What Is Good | 124
Conclusion | 128

About the Author | 135
Bibliography | 137

Foreword by Albert Hung

People like Dominic are a rare gift to the church. As an entrepreneur, real-estate consultant, and public servant, he brings a wealth of practical knowledge and real-world experience into complex conversations about how property assets can be utilized to support the mission of the church. Dominic understands that by loving God and serving our neighbors, we can also advance the common good. He's right: in a world torn by strife, each local church can show the beauty of Jesus' self-sacrificial love by blessing others.

Dominic is a committed disciple of Jesus with a solid grasp of Scripture, theology, and our current religious landscape. Despite the challenges facing the church, Dominic believes that our best days are before us—if we are willing to surrender our agendas (and our buildings) to God for the sake of the gospel. As an ecclesial overseer with responsibility for more than ninety congregations, many of which are struggling to remain vibrant and relevant, I find myself reaching out to Dominic on a near-weekly basis for prayer, counsel, and encouragement. Everyone who cares about the future of the church needs a friend and partner like Dominic in their corner.

Dominic and I often talk about making the most of the second half of life. When you realize that you have fewer years ahead than you do behind, your priorities become less about what you accomplish and accumulate and more about what you will give away and do to "spur others on toward love and good deeds" (Heb

10:24, NIV). We experience a growing desire to invest our God-given talents and treasures in the next generation, to plant trees under whose shade we will never sit.

As a pastor, I've had the privilege of having end-of-life conversations with many wonderful, godly people. We take time to celebrate the many good things that God allowed them to enjoy and the work they were privileged to do for his sake. Often, these kind saints will talk about their concern for their local church. They have watched the congregation dwindle over time. They are saddened by the conspicuous absence of young people. They wonder if there's anything that can be done. And on more than one occasion, these dear friends have looked at me and said, "Pastor, God has been so good to me, and I want others to be blessed like I have. I want to see my church full of life again. How can I help make that happen?"

When people are nearing the final chapter of their lives, they need two kinds of guides. They need a pastor, someone who will shepherd them in their twilight years, assure them of the hope we have in Christ, and help them discern what it means to finish well. They also need someone who can help them put their affairs in order. Is it time to downsize? Where will they live? To whom should they leave their estate? How can they be a blessing, even in death? For followers of Jesus, these are more than practical concerns—they are spiritual conversations.

In the same way, every church will eventually enter the second half of its natural life. When this happens, we need not be afraid. There are people who can help guide us, both spiritually and practically, so that we make the most of our time and resources in order to finish well. A church's second half may last several years, often a decade or more. But we should plan for the eventuality that one day, the assets God has entrusted to us will be given to a new generation, just as another generation once, as an act of faith and stewardship, entrusted them to us.

Throughout my lifetime, I have lived in twenty-two dwellings of various sizes, in fourteen cities, and in three countries. The house my family lives in now will not be our last. Over the years, it's become clear to me that where we live doesn't matter so much as who is with us on the journey. We've made memories in every single home, but we've held onto them lightly. When they have served their purposes, we give thanks and move on. It's people that matter.

Dominic understands the emotional significance we attach to church buildings. But he is calling us to hold onto them lightly and keep our eyes on what is most important: the redemptive mission of the church to reconcile a broken world to God through Christ. Toward that end, this book will help pastors, church leaders, and laypeople engage in hope-filled conversation about how to steward and leverage their property assets in ways that foster new life for our congregations and communities. We are praying for you. May your church be yet one more example of the resurrection power of Christ.

Acknowledgements

FIRST AND FOREMOST, I need to acknowledge God's active grace and mercy in my life. For reasons that I will never quite fathom, I was drawn to God's unconditional love, and I'm forever thankful to Mike "Easy Money" Madreau for introducing me to God in a way that only Mike could have. It worked, and it changed my life forever.

I want to thank my parents, John A. and Bernadine F. Dutra, for not only putting up with my hell-raising years, but also for financing my way through community college and an undergraduate and post-graduate experience at Santa Clara University. This education put me on the path toward future success in so many ways, and none of it would have been possible without them.

Thank you to my special teachers, Dr. Nagel, Mildred White, my ethics professor at Santa Clara University, and many others, who inspired me to read, think, and write. I'm especially thankful to Dr. Frank Rogers Jr. and Muriel Bernice Roberts, Professor of Spiritual Formation and Narrative Pedagogy at Claremont School of Theology, who inspired me through a spiritual retreat (Compassion-Based Social Engagement) to understand the need to make my faith real through active engagement with a hurting world. In truth, I've been most inspired by Frank's modeling of just such a life.

Frank introduced me to Ulrike Guthrie, my first true editor. Ulrike was so gracious to spend the time to read my material and begin to point me to what it really took to write a basic book proposal. More importantly, she told me the truth in love—that my book was going to need to "drastically" change and even noted that much of my work appeared "tortured" when initially presented to publishers. Ulrike believed in my message and stuck with me long enough to make perhaps the most important introduction; Steve Bohannon.

Steve is really the co-author of this book. From the beginning, he believed in my vision for unleashing faith-based real property for the furtherance of God's kingdom on earth. None of this book would have been possible without his brilliant editing, writing, and inspiration with the help of his editing partner Jolyon G. R. Pruszinski, PhD. I'm forever thankful to God for allowing me to be engaged in this process with such a talented team of writers. Steve, you've become so much more than an editor. You have become an inspiring brother in Christ.

Steve introduced me to my development editor, Joy Beth Smith. Joy Beth, you are what I'd call the "real deal." You've taught me so much about what it means to not only write a book, but to present it to the world in a way that I truly hope is compelling. Your joy and excitement inspire me every day. I could never thank you enough and am excited to take this future journey together.

I would be remiss to not express my profound appreciation to those leaders in the faith-based world that molded me into who I am today and were the inspirations for this book. Sister Elaine Marie Sanchez, Sister Sharon Flanigan and Sister Gladys Guenther were three presidents of the Sisters of the Holy Family, with whom I worked over the last thirty-plus years. They are all courageous and selfless leaders that were committed to creating and implementing a strategic plan for their portfolio of real property assets and doing so in a way that would bless future generations for years to come. They did so even though there was no clear plan or guide for doing so and, most inspiring, knowing that they themselves would not be there to gain recognition for these good works. You took a chance on me and faithfully worked with me over the years and showed me what it means to be a courageous and visionary faith-based leader.

Over this same thirty-plus years, I've had the privilege of working with and befriending Sister Linda Orrick. She is not only one of the most brilliant business and real-estate minds I know (she has an MBA from Notre Dame), but she has become both a sister and mentor to me. We have breakfast every month, and every time I talk too much. But she listens to me patiently and offers profoundly wise and compassionate advice. Sister Linda . . .you make my life a joy and I'm blessed to know you and call you my friend. My own pastor, Dr. Greg Roth, demonstrated what it means to be an "outward-facing" church through his active leadership in both our church and our community. And District Superintendent Albert Hung of the Northern California District of the Church of the Nazarene has become a spiritual mentor and inspiration of what it means to lead ministry in the twenty-first century.

Finally, I want to thank my wife of thirty-five years, Lisa. You are my greatest love, and life would not be the same without you. You've been with me through undergraduate and graduate school, five different companies that I've led and/or founded, two terms on a city council, life as an adjunct professor, and now as an author. You've never complained, and you've always been my greatest cheerleader and supporter. I love you with all my heart.

Introduction

If we don't change direction soon,
we'll end up where we're going.

—Irwin Corey

A friend of mine recently told me about his experience at a state-level pastor's conference. Dozens of Christian leaders joined together to focus on issues facing the local church. As the conference began, a phone rang. After an awkward pause and a few polite laughs, the speaker moved on.

A minute or two later, another phone rang out.

Then another.

Within the first fifteen minutes of the conference, a steady stream of phones chimed, buzzed, and chirped across the room. Within an hour, more than half the room was empty as many were outside on their phones, handling pressing church business.

I can count on one hand how many pastors tell me they have the space and time to pray, brainstorm, and strategically plan for the long-term vitality of their church. *There's always another call.*

When pastors are available to their congregants, it's beautiful and symbiotic, truly a picture of Christ and the church. But most of these shepherds are overworked, exhausted, underpaid, and facing expectations to grow a church that, if the statistics are to be believed, is likely shrinking. If you're in a ministry position, you know this well. As your brother in the Lord, I see you and your struggle. And, more importantly, God sees you.

This book is an invitation to *hope again* in the God who comforts the weak, raises the dead, and offers sufficient grace for each unique moment in the life of God's people, especially if we are willing to walk new paths.

Crossroads, Not Dead Ends

The Gospel of Luke's story of the Emmaus Road tells of two disciples commiserating after Jesus' death. The risen Christ joined them without revealing his identity, listening as they discussed their sadness and doubt. How could the Messiah be cut off from life by Jewish leaders under order of their Roman overlords? Jesus revealed a hidden truth as he explained how they had misunderstood the nature of his mission. After all, Jesus was always to be a suffering Messiah. As they sat down to eat, the pieces fell into place: the suffering Messiah was now the vindicated Lord and was in their presence. What appeared to be Christ's failure was the path to resurrection life. That's the payoff for us today: when we follow in Christ's path of self-sacrificial suffering for others, obstacles are cleared, new insight and purpose are given, and we discover *authentic, resurrection life* along the way. Failures are transformed. Death isn't an end.

The calls my pastor friend and his colleagues received at that conference were from church secretaries, deacons, spouses, and denominational leaders. Those calls ultimately stemmed from the same question: "What are we going to do?"

It was March of 2020, and the state had announced massive restrictions on public gatherings. Sunday services were to be canceled. COVID-19 was racing across the globe, and it was no longer safe to gather. How can a shepherd care for sheep they cannot see?

Since the beginning of the pandemic, we have come to a greater understanding about our vulnerabilities, both spiritually and physically. In our exhaustion, we look to the Lord for direction. Our services have fewer worshipers. Our neighbors are suffering and seem less interested in faith, at least in its American expression. Our church budgets are even tighter—and often giving is less than expected.

I'll readily admit that this book is *not* a comprehensive answer key to the troubling questions facing the Western church today. But I do know that in God's economy, our inadequacies are used to make us dependent on the Spirit, who speaks to us in a still small voice (1 Kgs 19:12). The nature of our faith remains the same, for Christ does not change.

An Invitation

I believe we are all being called to discern God's answers to the questions that every generation of believers must ask anew. "What is the Spirit saying to the church today? How does God want us to navigate our world now?"

Personally, I was wrestling with these big questions long before COVID-19, primarily because of my work. As President and CEO of Dutra Realty, I managed a team of nearly three hundred real estate professionals and staff, making our company one of the most successful real estate brokerages in the country. As an elected community leader, I began to recognize that educational institutions, faith-based communities, governmental agencies, and nonprofits were failing to fulfill their missions. Many were struggling financially or experiencing the pull of mission drift as they attempted to keep their doors open and services available. I came to realize that my knowledge of real estate could be a huge asset to these struggling organizations, so I founded a company that focused on helping community organizations fulfill their missions by utilizing real estate to become more financially stable.

For the past few decades as a real-estate consultant, I've been serving leaders of dying congregations as they decide how to use their property in ways that make the most sense for their specific situations. For the scores of closing local churches, I often can be perceived as playing the role of an undertaker. As churches decline, church leaders call me to help them decide how to handle the sale of their property. Almost daily I hear from a new pastor: *How do I go about selling our building? I never thought that I'd ask this question, but my congregation is dying.*

But over the years, just as the travelers on the Road to Emmaus, I've come to understand that what can be perceived as a death of a church is an amazing opportunity for rebirth. In fact, this message of life resurrected from the throes of death is at the heart of the Christian faith.

In the most recent stretch of my career, I've experienced the privilege of assisting church leaders as their congregation comes to an end. I've become their trusted advisor as I help them see more clearly how their real estate can be a fount of hope as they assess their options for the future. They see and feel the passion I have about the opportunities for growth that often follow death. And they inevitably come to embrace this same vision and hope. In that way, my role is akin to that of a master gardener, helping churches cultivate their land and usher in new life through renewed use of property, most often for larger, previously unimagined kingdom purposes. "Very truly I tell you, unless a kernel of wheat falls to the ground and dies, it remains only a single seed. But if it dies, it produces many seeds." (John 12:24 NIV).

This book outlines three ways churches can reimagine their mission through merging, leasing, or selling. Each section of this book retells the experiences of various congregations that have gone through one or more of these processes. These churches have done the hard work of dying to their own deflating dreams and goals to serve the greater church by using their space differently or giving it up altogether. We can learn so much from these stories about how our local churches don't have to die alone and without having impacted a suffering world that so longs for the love of God. There is a different, life-sustaining path.

These courageous leaders and fading congregations are choosing to *not* go on life support. They are choosing to *not* use their dwindling resources to comfortably support themselves as their remaining congregants fade away. Facing shrinking budgets and membership rosters, they are choosing to walk with the Spirit in a renewed posture of faithful reliance and intentional, outward-facing missional practice. Every single one of them heard a calling from the Spirit to act out God's love for the life of their neighbors—and thus, the world. So, with faith and imagination, they are moving towards their communities, serving them, and inviting them to share their lives, their spaces, and the wealth of their real property resources.

As I've witnessed this extraordinary movement of God in many different faith contexts, I've come to believe that more congregations should prayerfully explore if they are called to take this path. By implementing the missionally driven real-estate strategies of merging with another congregation, leasing out space, or selling altogether, congregations have a chance to move with God in deeper ways.

No matter the size of a declining church, every congregational leader has the chance to rally their people, calling them to look out from the place God has brought them and envision a further land of promise. The congregation may not fully arrive, but through intentional, spiritually rich practices and service, the life of Christ can be shared in new, thoughtful ways. In the words of the ancient philosopher Seneca, "We should strive, not to live long, but to live rightly."[1]

Living—and Dying—Rightly

Granted, there are a lot of books that suggest ways for churches to revitalize. Even before our national crises, many of you probably read books about transformational churches, turnaround churches, and visionary leadership. While sometimes inspiring,

1. Seneca, *Epistles 93–124*, 3.

those visions are too often byproducts of what Eugene Peterson calls the "Americanization" of the church, in which churches are treated like businesses that cater to the religious needs of their consumer base.[2] That gimmicky, consumer-driven model is not the way forward. Most church redevelopment literature starts off by wrongly assuming every struggling church needs to live.

That may sound caustic. But track with me: why must a dying church survive?

Why put a congregation on inwardly focused hospice care if they are hoarding wealth and space? How does it benefit the kingdom of God when a dozen congregants refuse to lend out their large building? How can such a congregation justify "living" when financially struggling minority churches down the street are growing but have limited space?

Let me put it even more broadly, even for larger, more sustainable churches: how can we justify not sharing buildings that remain unoccupied six days a week?

In many cases, children in our surrounding neighborhoods don't have a safe place to be cared for in after-school programs. Unhoused neighbors sit on the street, stifling in the heat. Yet we turn them away and keep the doors of our empty buildings closed over 80 percent of the week. Why? Because we are missing something.

My intention in writing this book is not to increase your membership or giving. It's not to buy your aging congregation another five or ten years. No, I believe that God is calling the church to die to self when facing organizational decline or collapse. And it's only as leaders guide their congregations to self-denial and outward-focused mission that God's plans for restoration and renewal can truly be implemented at the local level. Here's the gospel paradox: along this path of death, individual congregations taste the resurrection life of God.

I am joining a chorus of voices calling the church back to the divine mandate to pursue God's mission in the world. By re-envisioning why we do church in the first place, we can move past

2. Peterson, *Practice Resurrection*, 23–24.

the presumption that dying churches should be placed in hospice care as they dwindle down to a few members. As Christians, we cannot be in the business of making nearly dead institutions comfortable, just because they used to be a source of life. There is a way to appropriately cherish the past without allowing it to cloud our perspective of God's true call to the members of your congregation. This is a call to embrace new life through selfless services of others, which is especially important when you consider that the median age in most of our churches is over fifty years old. By embracing God's call these same members can find a new raison raison d'être in the remaining twenty to thirty years of their lives.

This book offers one main argument, which, while simple, is radical for many churches: real estate and church mission can and should go together. The church has wealth in the form of real estate that can be used in service to God's glorious, life-giving missional plans, even when a church is coming to the end of its life cycle.

While this book is about a renewed use of real estate, it is not just about the formal process of signing a lease or selling a property—it's about mission. It isn't just about *how* churches have gone through processes of merging, selling, or leasing—it's about *why.*

After providing a larger theological picture of my understanding of the why, I will share stories of faithful communities who have accepted the invitation to journey with God in a new direction. At the very least, I hope to gently urge you, your congregation, and your denominational administrators towards a more missional use of your real estate. I hope the stories you discover in this book empower you to implement Scripturally rooted, practically minded innovations in your own context.

1

To Live Is Christ, To Die Is Gain

The truth does not change according to our ability to stomach it.

—Flannery O'Connor

I fondly remember spending an extended season in France with my wife, Lisa, in the late eighties, while we worked for a French construction company. The work was hard, but the time spent exploring the French countryside more than made up for it. Stateside church attendance was surging, so we were shocked to find that the large, historic churches that dotted the French landscape were nearly empty, locked up, or abandoned on Sunday mornings.

Where had the church members gone? Had they slowly died off, never to be replaced by a new generation of believers? Had they left in droves as secularism took firm hold across Europe? When we asked, we were met with puzzled looks, shrugs, or silence. Not many people seemed to care.

Discouraged, it took us months to find and join a community of believers. The small Baptist church met in a plain building—a stark contrast to the beautiful, ancient Parisian cathedrals. Our congregation was dwarfed by the crowds we saw on historic church tours. Despite the humble size of our church, we found joy and contentment during our time abroad.

When we returned to the United States, I sensed a growing disillusionment among those who attended mainline and Catholic churches, and I couldn't help but notice the sea of silver and grey hair each week as we worshiped at our church. In conversations with my brothers and sisters in Christ, I learned they were growing weary, ready to pass the torch to a younger generation that was largely missing.

This announcement shouldn't have been a surprise as our church community struggled throughout the 1990s. The trends became more pronounced over time: younger generations were absent from church each week, choosing not to replicate their parents' faith journeys. Our experience was representative of larger national trends. Consistent polling during the last two decades has confirmed that a decline in church attendance has continued unabated.[1] Churches in the United States are well on the way to following their European counterparts.

Richard Rohr suggests that the solidarity previously provided by life in church community is now being replaced by participation in "think tanks, support groups, prayer groups, study groups, projects building houses for the poor, healing circles, or mission organizations." Interestingly, for Rohr, this isn't problematic. He believes Christians aren't leaving the church and giving up on faith altogether. Rather, they are "realigning with groups that live Christian values in the world, instead of just gathering to again hear the readings, recite the creed, and sing songs on Sunday."[2] If embraced, this could be a path toward an inspired new life.

Ultimately, the health of a church isn't found in numbers. Large churches aren't always healthy, and small churches aren't necessarily failing. Some organized groups of believers remain small. Some grow slowly over time, as they actively work out their faith. God waters the seeds and expands the kingdom as they move into the community. These kinds of small (but steadily growing)

1. Jones, "U.S. Church Membership Falls."

2. Rohr, *Universal Christ*, 200.

churches are healthy precisely because they are vibrant in things of the Lord. They serve one another, work to meet the needs of their neighbors, and creatively welcome people that look and think differently.

But the other side of the "church size" coin is more my focus here. I worry about the churches that do not grow—the churches that, though they may be bigger, are not vibrant in spiritual health because they expend their energies *looking inward.* I want to address the church leaders and denominational-level overseers of these types of churches—those whose congregations are not growing but have long ago peaked and are now slowly fading.

As I think back to those beautiful, unoccupied church buildings across France, I wonder how church leaders felt as they watched their congregations shrink. When did they realize their organizational lives were over? Did they regret leaving a legacy of little more than crumbling walls and fading memories? And how do we measure the health and vitality of a church before it's too late?

I've discovered that church leaders often don't realize they need help. Many churches assume things are okay because attendance is high enough, the offering plates are relatively full, and there's a smattering of young faces in the aging crowd. There may be discussion about hiring a new youth pastor, but larger ministry strategies stay the same. Outreach is limited, especially as the demographics of the neighborhood change, and the church is built around programs rather than reaching and serving people. We as congregants don't sense the danger in plateauing because churches are our homes, providing our greatest sense of community. The respite and resources we receive there can make us blind to the cracks developing in the metaphorical (or even physical) walls. And this is, sadly, a common occurrence.

"It is rare for a long-term church member to see erosion in his or her church. Growth may come rapidly, but decline is usually slow, imperceptibly slow," argues Thom Rainer.

> Often the decline is in the physical facilities, but it is much more than that. The decline is in the vibrant

> ministries that once existed. The decline is in the prayer lives of the members who remain. The decline is in the outward focus of the church. The decline is in the connection with the community. The decline is in the hopes and dreams of those who remain.[3]

We love the comfort and stability of what we know, but that comfort can be deceptive. While often counterintuitive and in open conflict with our aversion to change, the church isn't called to live in comfort but to pursue the self-giving mission of God. This is where new life is found.

In my work as a real-estate consultant and broker, some of the more tragic stories I hear from dying churches involve remaining members who are in a state of denial. Despite numbers declining, buildings in disrepair, and shrinking staff, these congregants tell themselves that things will get better, or, even worse, they honestly believe that things are fine. This results in a death grip on their properties and a desperate attempt to retain the status quo. They may make half-hearted attempts to adjust to a new and changing world, but these responsibilities are often placed on the shoulders of the existing pastor, or a new pastor who will make all things better. Often, these men and women don't know how to move forward; they are stuck in a state of grief over the loss of the past and are unable to identify what's missing from their culture and mission. In most cases, fear of the unknown causes them to resist the need to honestly address the spiritual dangers of continuing as things are.

As I've met more and more members of now-defunct churches, I see a similar pattern: the congregation thought things were relatively stable, and then suddenly, without much warning, things plummeted. After a series of downward spirals, the church could no longer sustain itself, and the decision was made to close. I hear the sorrow in their voices. What lies under the surface in nearly every case is a shared set of congregational characteristics. Comfortable, plateaued churches have:

3. Rainer, *Autopsy*, locs. 26–27.

1. A limited sense of mission.
2. A lack of awareness about their position within the surrounding community.
3. A sense of nostalgia for a bygone era.

Fading congregations become known less for community involvement and more for an entrenched fortress mentality. There is a shift from self-sacrifice to self-preservation. Rainer notes, "The most pervasive and common thread of our autopsies was that the deceased churches lived for a long time with the past as hero. They held on more tightly with each progressive year. They often clung to things of the past with desperation and fear." Perhaps most damning of Rainer's assessments: "When any internal or external force tried to change the past, they responded with anger and resolution: 'We will die before we change.'"[4]

According to significant studies conducted in recent years, 80–85 percent of churches in North America are either plateaued or tracking downward.[5] We can put it even more concretely than that. Rainer has calculated that "as many as 100,000 churches in America are showing signs of decline toward death."[6] To not accept that the church, writ large, is at a historic crossroads is the definition of an unhealthy state of denial.

The implications of these figures are staggering. If true, this means four out of five community churches are somewhere in the process of moving towards organizational death. As we continue to feel the full impact of the COVID-19 pandemic, my sense is that more churches are in danger than ever before.

What else can we learn from these statistics? Interestingly, per the same survey, the 14 percent of congregations that are actively growing are not typically white, nor part of a mainline Protestant

4. Rainer, *Autopsy*, loc. 33.
5. Malphurs, "State of the American Church"
6. Rainer, *Autopsy*, loc. 19.

congregation. These growing communities are largely younger and more demographically diverse. How we welcome and accept that reality is a sign of our own spiritual maturity. Yonkman reminds us that "No time machine exists that will bring the United States and its mainline churches back to the 1950s—which for many churches were the glory years. Declining churches can be restored to a life-giving, life-changing relationship with God, but the relationship will not look and feel the same as it did before."[7] This is the heart of the resurrection story.

I love the faithful, hope-filled categories that Mark Elsdon uses to re-describe our moment: "Membership and giving may have declined, but God has not declined. God's love, God's justice, God's care for all creation is as strong as it has always been. God is at work in the world right now with all of what we have and despite all of what we perceive to be missing."[8]

Grabbing onto that reality is comforting to me. God is still God. When I lose sight of this, it's too easy to hang my head and think that God has somehow forgotten the faithful. But God is up to something. To step into God's future, we must first accept where we are. We must recognize and acknowledge the problem before we can decide on the best course of action. The church can continue to fulfill the promises of the gospel if she is willing to envision a reimagined faith. God is inviting us to be a part of a new thing, and that should fill us with hope.

Here are four questions to answer if you are discerning whether you are leading a dying congregation:

1. Are most of your members retired?

According to Pew Research, mainline Protestant adults in the United States have a median age of fifty-two, higher than the group's median age in 2007 (fifty) and older than any other major religious tradition. This is reflective of current societal trends where large

7. Yonkman, *Reconstructing Church*, 38.

8. Elsdon, *We Aren't Broke*, 166.

numbers of Baby Boomers are entering their retirement years. The reason this is bad news is that mainline Protestants have one of the lowest retention rates of any major religious tradition. Less than half of those raised in the faith are continuing to identify with it as adults. For every convert to mainline Protestantism, about 1.7 people have left the mainline tradition behind.[9] At this point, there doesn't appear to be any sufficient "youth movement" to stop the overall decline in membership and engagement.

Consider your own church. What is the median age? How siloed are your generations in their activities, Bible studies, and classes? What is the largest growing demographic in your congregation?

2. Are your youth and young adult ministries thriving?

The downward trend in church attendance appears destined to continue as young people no longer attend church as their parents did. They are becoming increasingly unaffiliated. Young adults are particularly unlikely to stay with mainline churches—just 37 percent of millennials who were raised in the mainline tradition still identify with Protestantism.[10] Among millennial adults (born since 1981), only 11 percent are mainline Protestants. Gallup surveys make clear that the Catholic Church has similar challenges, with only one-fourth claiming to have attended church in the last seven days (as opposed to almost half for those over sixty years of age).[11]

Gallup notes that "All of this comes amid a broader trend of more Americans opting out of formal religion or being raised without it altogether."[12] In 2016, Gallup found one in five Ameri-

9. "Religious Switching and Intermarriage," fig. 1.

10. Lipka, "Mainline Protestants," paras. 5, 7, fig. 2.

11. Saad, "Catholics' Church Attendance," fig. 2.

12. Saad, "Catholics' Church Attendance," para. 18.

cans professing no religious identity, up from as little as 2 percent just over sixty years ago.[13]

Does your church see a large drop-off from youth ministry to young couples? How do you make space for twenty- and thirty-somethings in your congregation? How do you equip middle and high school students to own their faith and continue to invest in their church families?

3. As you look out at your congregation, is nearly everyone white?

As the United States grows more racially and ethnically diverse, mainline Protestant churches remain almost entirely white. Only 6 percent of mainline congregations are Latino, 3 percent are Black, and 1 percent are Asian. This does not bode well. According to a 2008 article in the *New York Times*, data from the US census can be used to calculate that by 2042, Americans who identify themselves as Hispanic, Black, Asian, American Indian, Native Hawaiian and Pacific Islander will together outnumber non-Hispanic whites. For the first time, both the number and the proportion of non-Hispanic whites, who now account for 66 percent of the population, will decline, starting around 2030. By 2050, their share will dip to 46 percent.[14]

Does your church reflect the community's demographics? Has your congregation grown and expanded with the changing national data? Are you intentionally finding ways to incorporate and celebrate this diversity, or is it allowed to exist at best?

4. Are your budgets tightening? Is giving gradually down?

Simple math tells us that if the total number of church attendees is declining, then the number of donations will follow. This trend is

13. Newport, "Five Key Findings on Religion in the U.S."
14. Roberts, "Census Bureau Gives the Melting Pot a Stir," paras. 2, 9.

even more pronounced with younger generations who are not as familiar with or encumbered by the notion of tithing. Compounding these problems further are the growing donations for charitable giving that siphon away church contributions.

Is your church experiencing more of an ebb than a flow to your finances? In what areas do you see financial growth? Where are you thriving and where are you dying?

❧

I readily admit that there are real socioeconomic forces that impact the nature of any local church's ministry. There are demographic shifts, seasons of economic constriction and decline, and a whole host of difficult cultural issues that impact congregants and the church.[15] However, I am convinced that the church *can* and *should* adapt to meet the unique challenges of our season.

In his letter to the church at Rome, Paul strongly asserted that we must "know the time" because our salvation is "nearer than when we first believed" (Rom 13:11 NKJV). Paul did not suggest adaptation that compromises to the evil days. Instead, we must all learn to prayerfully discern our context and to continue to act out Christ's calling. Foundational to the context of Paul's command (to know the time) is the command to love our neighbors, which Paul says is the fulfillment of the law (Rom 13:10).

No matter our context, the way to fulfill God's commands is to love our neighbors in a self-sacrificial, genuine way. As we adapt to the challenges of our time, we must continue to do so in this spirit—and to make sure that we stay aligned with the ancient standards of Christ. There is continuity even in adaptation.

Scott Cormode says, "practices embody beliefs,"[16] and we naturally reflect what we understand. We must connect renewed church life with mission in meaningful ways to those outside the doors of our church. But before we can move forward, we must

15. Jones, *Facing Decline, Finding Hope*, xv.

16. Cormode, *Innovative Church*, 79 (emphasis in original).

fully acknowledge that we're struggling. We must begin the process of letting go, so that we can stop "strangling [the] church."[17]

Reframing Death Through the Lens of Stewardship

In our culture, we glamorize the young, healthy, and strong. With rare exceptions, images of the sick, elderly, and dying are relegated to spaces that we avoid at all costs. "Pity them, but don't be like them," our culture advises at every turn. Perhaps this is one of the reasons that we are all so resistant to speaking honestly to each other about our declining numbers, limited outreach events, and largely ineffective ministries.

In fact, the fundamental roadblock standing in the way of our future as God's people is denial. L. Gail Irwin suggests that "denial indicates that the psyche is unable to integrate the reality of change or loss at the speed that change is occurring. In some people, a sort of 'freezing' occurs that renders them unable to adjust their behavior to new circumstances." I believe our denial is directly related to our lack of mindful presence in our daily lives.[18]

It's human nature to lash out or tune out when someone brings up our faults. But as David Benner helps us see, our spiritual lives demand a commitment to reality: we are dependent on God's word to see things as they truly are.[19] Trusting God means accepting reality and living in light of it.

There is freedom in owning our inadequacies because it forces us to return our focus on the omniscience of an all-loving God. There is peace in embracing failure. And only in doing both things, along with developing a keen awareness of our strengths and contributions, can we prayerfully discern with our brothers and sisters what the Spirit is saying to the church. We must wholeheartedly accept that there is "no condemnation to those who are in Christ Jesus" (Rom 8:1, NKJV). Because we are named as God's beloved,

17. Rendle, "Legacy Conversation," para. 4.

18. Irwin, *Toward the Better Country*, 25.

19. Benner, *Gift of Being Yourself*, 58.

there is hope. Despite our struggles now, God is ready for us to meet this moment. Let us remember to be inspired by the wisdom of 2 Cor 7:10: "For godly sorrow produces repentance leading to salvation, not to be regretted; but the sorrow of the world produces death" (NKJV).

Death is universal. Psychiatrist Elizabeth Kübler-Ross gives us a model for the process of grief most people experience when facing the death of a loved one. This fivefold process is a cyclical transition from denial to anger to bargaining to depression to acceptance.[20]

Dying congregations often exhibit similar patterns of grief when facing the impending end of their organizational religious life. People react with outright denial and anger at the suggestion that their future as a church is limited. When pastors attempt to steer their dying churches towards using their facilities to bless other believers in younger, thriving churches, such advice is regularly rejected. The few remaining members hunker down and refuse to surrender what they believe is "their" space, feeling the risks greatly outweigh any potential benefit. For aging members, fears of one's own impending death are frequently tied up with the refusal to accept the demise of the church, complicating things further.

We need not overlook these realities. We serve a God of resurrection and life eternal, so we do not need to fear the end of a season in our earthly work. When the light of Christ shines on such fears, things can look different—as does the path forward.

In Reverend Albert Hung's current position as District Superintendent of the Northern California District Church of the Nazarene, he oversees scores of small, struggling churches. Too often, he says, congregations conduct conversations about closing their church in what are perceived as cold, business-like terms. But this isn't just a matter of logistics and legal agreements. Instead, it should be a

20. Kübler-Ross, *On Death and Dying*.

truly spiritual thing to think about the death of a church and the corresponding sale of a church building.

Fear of loss, Reverend Hung says, is natural. But by reconsidering what lies behind it, healing can occur, and the mission of Christ can be furthered rather than destroyed. One of the most helpful ways to consider this is by reclaiming the Scriptural calling of stewardship.

Stewardship is a loaded concept, theologically speaking. Mark DeYmaz teaches us that while stewardship typically denotes fiscal responsibility, "going forward, our understanding of good stewardship should also include the biblical expectation of knowing what to do with the assets entrusted to us." DeYmaz's conclusion is pointed: "Pastors and churches can no longer afford to sit on their assets!"[21]

Our personal frameworks of stewardship inform how we view and use our church spaces, whether our church is heading towards closure or not. Before any church can fruitfully decide on a path towards closure, our fundamental identity as Christ's people must be clarified, accepted, and celebrated. God gives us gifts. And we are to use them for Christ's glory and the world's good. We too often forget that, like the gift of grace, we originally received the gift of a gathering place, the local church. This space has been granted to us for a season, but not forever.

This feels backwards considering Western thought patterns and practices. Our overriding commitments should be to God's kingdom and how Jesus wants us to follow him. When we slip into secular categories of ownership or discourse about what's ours, we are not following the way of the king.

Change has come to us, whether we know it, like it, or want to admit it. And it will continue to come. But these changes—and our corresponding failures and spirals—are not a surprise to God. The One who knows all things has given us all that we need for life and godliness (2 Pet 1:3). Indeed, the apostle Peter helps us to see that because of God's gift of divine power and his incalculable promises, we can join with God (2 Pet 1:3–4). The "we" here is

21. DeYmaz, *Coming Revolution*, loc. 56.

the community of faith, the result of God's workmanship. God has prepared us for the "good works . . . so that we would walk in them" (Eph 2:10 NASB).

Even before our own struggles, failures, and resistance to change God has been at work to help us to overcome our fears and inadequacies. God is ready to grow us to more fully work out our salvation (Phil 2:12) and to live out the life of God to the world so that shalom of God will be cosmic in scope. To put it another way, "God is at work through the Spirit to create communities that prefigure and embody the reconciliation and healing of the world."[22]

As you read this description of God's action, you might be acknowledging it at some level, but the habit of acting on this truth makes the most basic parts of faith new and life-giving. As with the travelers on the road to Emmaus, what is right in front of our eyes is often too familiar to be of help.

I believe that leaning into a fuller story of our life with God requires not only accepting reality but also committing to trust God and each other. Learning to lean into this posture of faith takes practice done wholly within community. James K. A. Smith helpfully articulates the ways in which our Christian imagination is renewed and expanded in the context of ongoing liturgical practices. This formation is itself generative of the Christian's *habitus* in the world. Smith writes that "any missional, formative Christian institution that is bent on sending out *actors*—agents of reformation and renewal—will need to attend to the reformation of our *habitus*."[23]

Developing sustainable habits and truly missional churchly practices must be done in the shared space of communal life together.[24] As we learn to talk about our corporate life in Christ as the church, we feel less pressure. Acknowledging the elephant(s) in the room is a freeing experience. We aren't alone. In fact, our frank and humble admissions are one of the very means that we grow up in Christ. The way forward may feel counterintuitive, but it's

22. Hays, *Moral Vision of the New Testament*, 32.

23. Smith, *Imagining the Kingdom*, 157 (emphasis in original).

24. Bonhoeffer, *Life Together*.

Scriptural: repentance in community leads to restoration, growth, and wholeness. Luke tells us that we will even experience times of refreshing (Acts 3:19). What a hope-filled promise!

The very experience of speaking this way takes work. Young members of the church must be willing to listen to those who have spent years safeguarding the faith. And older members must be willing to hear where they have fallen short and welcome a new generation's ideas. There are plenty of practical ways to create shared spaces to listen, pray, think about, and study how God might have us manage the church's decline. In doing so, we will learn to see our corporate acknowledgement of the church's decline as a divine gift. It can be a unifying moment to come together and accept our current state. When we lay aside our finger-pointing, we can be one like Jesus prayed in the Gospel of John. As the apostle Paul said so long ago, we can face the death of those we love and that which we love and not mourn like those without hope (1 Thess 4:13).

As Christ's disciples, we are called to death—a willing, sacrificial, self-dying. Denial of self in pursuit of Christ is meant to be part of our very DNA, so by the Spirit's power, we can reimagine the death of the church through the lens of our calling as disciples. We can accept our decline and choose to die to self in service of God's larger mission.

Learning to Embrace a Different Kind of Death

In the days leading up to his own inevitable arrest and death, Jesus told his followers that "unless a grain of wheat falls into the earth and dies, it remains alone" (John 12:24 NASB). The path to fruit comes through an intentional, beautiful, self-giving kind of death. This death doesn't look like that of the church's slow decline and demise. It's the difference between a building manager refusing to replace dead smoke detectors and a firefighter willingly entering that burning building and saving its occupants.

In the context of Jesus' own ministry, Jesus describes the path of his people in terms of denial of self and daily cross bearing (Luke

9:23–24). Jesus' calling was not morbid. It was not a navel-gazing, self-immolating, and solely heavenly-minded way of thinking. Rather, it was an invitation to walk out a path that Jesus himself blazed. Through his suffering, he brought life.

In case this sounds foreign or idealistic, think of self-death through the lens of priorities and personal attachments. Anything we grab onto for its perceived life-giving properties must, according to Paul, be upended by our greater commitment to kingdom priorities, where peace, justice, and love dominate every aspect of life.

Look at the way Paul seamlessly ties these realities together in Romans 6: "So you too, consider yourselves to be dead to sin, but alive to God in Christ Jesus. Therefore, sin is not to reign in your mortal body so that you obey its lusts, and do not go on presenting the parts of your body to sin as instruments of unrighteousness; but present yourselves to God as those who are alive from the dead, and your body's parts as instruments of righteousness for God (vv. 11–13 NASB).

If a local church is dying, it may very well mean that the body is overcome with a series of debilitating illnesses. At root, far too few of us are willingly laying down our whole lives to become an "instrument of righteousness." Framing things this way sounds both familiar and radical, doesn't it? But no more radical than Jesus challenging Peter by asking him repeatedly if he truly loved him. If so, like Peter we are called to use all the church's resources, including its real estate, to feed God's sheep.

I'm convinced we so often miss Jesus' intentions in our personal lives and church ministries not only because of our stubbornness and fickle nature, but also because of our over-familiarity with Scripture.[25] In addition to having desensitized eyes and ears, we have inadvertently lost the force of Jesus' commands by practicing and prioritizing a comfortable, often self-serving way of being Christian. We love the American Dream, one that ends with certain victory that can be proudly displayed on the many social

25. Cartwight and Hulshof, *Everyday Bible Study*, 90.

media outlets which proclaim our success. But we are not called to the American Dream.

Too often, the North American church stands out as a negative contrast with the picture of community found in Scripture. We import Western ideas of ownership and autonomy into passages in Scripture, such as Paul's expression, "where the Spirit of the Lord is, there is freedom" (2 Cor 3:17 NASB). This verse is used most often to embrace selfish, self-serving ends, but in the very next verse, we learn that we are "being transformed into the same image from glory to glory, just as from the Lord, the Spirit" (2 Cor 3:18 NASB). The fruit of the Spirit, who is at work in us all, is to become like Jesus. To look like Jesus is not to grasp onto our own right, but to live an outwardly manifested love. We are not to be an island unto ourselves but to help carry another's burden (Gal 6:2). This means that we move out into the world to serve the unchurched. Our freedom in the Lord is meant to be a chance to creatively enact, with our full agency, what it means to be human. Loving outreach to the other is the hallmark of faith—not the closed-fist demand of our rights.

Since the Enlightenment, our default mode has been to privatize any expression of faith, thus routinely cutting off our shared life in Christ. But the truth is that our private lives impact our public spheres of influence. This doesn't look like a facile, gimmicky attempt to intellectually dominate or bring every person to where we stand. Genuine life with God pours out into the public sphere primarily in the form of charity and love. When we practice Jesus' words, we can't help but offer a beacon of light and hope as a city on a hill. Like Jesus' first followers, sometimes we need to be reminded that private, individual expressions of commitment are not enough.

To fully embrace such a pivot to the death of self requires ongoing discipleship. And following Jesus in the twenty-first century always involves long-term Christian practices, which themselves flow out of renewed affections. Cognitive shifts are just one small piece of the puzzle of Christian renewal. Professor James K. A. Smith puts it well:

> Discipleship is more a matter of hunger and thirsting than of believing and knowing. Jesus' command to follow him is a command to align our loves and longings with his—to want what God wants, to desire what God desires, to hunger and thirst after God and crave a world where he is all in all—a vision encapsulated by the shorthand 'kingdom of God.' Jesus is a teacher who doesn't just inform our intellect but forms our very loves. He isn't content to simply deposit new ideas into your mind; he is after nothing less than your wants, your loves, your longings.[26]

We can't conform to a few facts about life with God. We're talking about *Spiritual* (inferring work of the Holy Spirit) transformations that occur as we experience and more fully embrace the love of God in Christ.

David Brenner's work is helpful here. There is a difference, Brenner suggests, between our obedience to God's calling and our full-hearted surrender to the love of Jesus. "It is quite easy to obey God for the wrong reasons," he writes. "What God desires is submission of our heart and will, not simply compliance in our behavior."[27] To fully walk out the path that God has for us, we will need to see the world that we thought we understood in new, often unsettling, ways. Discipleship then begets an aesthetic—and even a church culture!—that is kingdom-like. Professor Smith puts it nicely: "It is not enough to have a Christian 'perspective' on the world; *we need nothing less than a Christian imagination.*"[28] Smith goes on:

> In sum, if we are going to be agents of the coming kingdom, *acting* in ways that embody God's desires for creation, then our imaginations need to be conscripted

26. Smith, *You Are What You Love*, 19–20.

27. Benner, *Surrender to Love*, 142.

28. Smith, *Imagining the Kingdom*, 157. Emphasis mine.

> by God. It is not enough to convince our intellects; our imaginations need to be caught by—and caught up into—the Story of God's restorative, reconciling grace for all of creation. It won't be enough for us to be convinced; we need to be *moved*.[29]

This formation-to-action does not happen overnight. And it does not happen in total isolation. Our growth on this path of discipleship happens especially as we interact with those around us—Christians, yes, but also with the public sphere. When we fail to do so well, it is inhibiting our ability to connect with a hurting world that is in desperate need of God's healing love.

The declining participation of Americans in church isn't just a story about the decline of organizations. Failing to gather, pray, confess, and worship as a community impacts the individual and larger spiritual ecosystem.[30] Those of us who worship week in and week out aren't free from blame. How often are we guilty of setting up our own petty kingdoms, or church cultures, of our own making? Without an eye to the full calling of the Lord, we inevitably circle back up, drawing up tighter and tighter group boundaries, excluding those that are outsiders. This is not the way of Christ. Dying churches are full of Westernized Christians who miss out on the corporate implications of our individual calling to dismiss personal interests in service of others.

It may be easy to read along with me and think *what about secular pressures on the church? Don't our busy lives, difficult work schedules, and changing ideas of norms and community boundaries play a role, too?* Perhaps. But it's not only our Western world that sets up roadblocks to our future with God. We must be honest with ourselves about our lack of commitment to discipleship and mission. We each have control issues, a tendency towards self-reliance, and a deep autonomous streak. These parts of us must die.

No dying church can just decide to have a new life and begin to flourish because of determination and grit. No church leader can will their way to a new, vibrant future. Every aspect of the vision

29. Smith, *Imagining the Kingdom*, 157. Emphasis in original.

30. Lowe and Lowe, *Ecologies of Faith*, 56–62.

I am laying out must be understood and implemented spiritually and organically. It is through the foundation of God's work, God's mission, and God's enabling call that we are to act out by faith. We must resist any urge to think so simplistically as to believe we can just follow some self-help guide and recover a church.

We belong to the vine, Christ, and any push forward that accepts the death of a church and practices self-dying must tap into Christ and not depart from him. The call to go with God in mission presupposes a deep, vital relationship with Christ. Within the context of John 15, Jesus frames this dynamic perfectly: "Apart from Me, you can do nothing."

As we abide in Jesus, we present our needs, and Jesus promises it will be done. This powerful picture is missing if a church of disciples cumulatively moves into a world in which they coast along, propelled by nothing but past relational power and a few wins in their programming or annual events. The call to live out of Christ's life is ongoing. When a ministry is entering its death throes as an organization, the invitation to die is not a final judgment. It is a grace-filled opportunity to consider what new life God offers through embracing the full range of his commands and possible options.

This allows and requires us to let go of the past. Our survival as a local church organization is far less important than our fidelity to the full expression of Christ's kingdom. Living out a sense of abundance takes faith, knowing that the church that turns to Christ will receive all things it needs, as God sees fit.

On this new path, life emerges.

Living the Resurrection Life of Christ

If the first roadblock in the life of God's people is our inability to accept our status as a dying church, the second might be our own lack of sharing the abundant life of the Triune God with others. If "what we love defines us,"[31] the ethos of our church within the

31. Smith, *You Are What You Love.*

community is telling. In a toxic and divided world that is starving for a life-giving, loving relationship with others and God, we have an opportunity to be a blessing. The Master shares his very Spirit with us and sends us outwards for that very purpose—to share the life of Jesus.

Paul draws this out: the resurrection power of the Spirit is present in the body of Christ. "But if the Spirit of Him who raised Jesus from the dead dwells in you, He who raised Christ Jesus from the dead will also give life to your mortal bodies through His Spirit who dwells in you" (Rom 8:11 NASB).

Re-describing conditions through God's lens radically challenges how we move forward in action. For the Christian, death to self is never an end. We who follow Christ get a rich foretaste of the resurrection life and power of God in the present. The God who is making all things new is already in the business of sharing that kingdom with us *now*. That is why our work in the world matters.

By intentionally dying to self, we can live out of a resurrection life in ways that serve the missional purposes of God. As we willfully entrust our individual and corporate lives to Christ, we quickly experience the love of God in new ways. Our old, self-focused natures begin to fade, and we become concerned for the welfare of others. We begin to truly experience the abundant life for which Jesus came and inhabited our world. Isn't that the way Paul describes our relationship to the resurrected Christ?

> With humility consider one another as more important than yourselves; do not merely look out for your own personal interests, but also for the interests of others. Have this attitude in yourselves which was also in Christ Jesus, who, as He already existed in the form of God, did not consider equality with God something to be grasped, but emptied Himself by taking the form of a bond-servant and being born in the likeness of men. And being found in appearance as a man, He humbled Himself by becoming obedient to the point of death: death on a cross. (Phil 2:3–8 NASB)

As Richard Hays points out when reflecting on this passage, "Christ's obedience to the point of death (2:8) is offered to the Philippians as a pattern for their own obedience (2:12). Just as he obediently suffered, so the Philippians should stand firm in the gospel, even when it requires them to suffer (1:27–30)."[32]

When we talk about personal growth, it involves not only an end of one way of living but a new, natural preoccupation with outward-facing service. Michael Gorman says, "To put it simply: the cross of Christ reveals a missional, justifying, justice-making God and creates a missional, justified, justice-making people."[33]

Discipleship is the opposite of surviving. It is radically teleological (understanding our design and purpose in the material world). We live to give to and for the point of self-offering. Paul described his own ministry and service to the church this way: "But even if I am being poured out as a drink offering upon the sacrifice and service of your faith, I rejoice and share my joy with you all" (Phil 2:17 NASB). And so, the church can continually and practically revisit one essential question: who are we becoming as a church?

This is a way of living out the full facets of God's reconciling work. We're always in a state of repentance for the things we've done and left undone.

But the church is not the sum of its failures. The church has the potential to be a life-giving force of love, joy, peace, and generosity in a world that needs healing.

32. Hays, *Moral Vision*, 29.

33. Gorman, *Becoming the Gospel*, 9.

2

A Call to Jubilee

Remember how the resurrected Christ confronted the disciples when they had returned to old habits in the familiar surroundings of their hometown. Jesus pointedly referred to familiar surroundings, comfortable routines, and long-time friendships—and then asked the disciples if they love him more than those things.

—Thomas G. Bandy and Page M. Brooks

If we are willing to learn, God wants to correct our mistaken ideas about death and teach us what life in Christ looks like. Since the mission of Christ is itself the extension of God's work with and for Israel, it shouldn't be any surprise that the new life that God calls us to share in is deeply aligned with the Old Testament. The good news of Jesus stands in continuity with Israel's faith and hope.

Throughout the Old Testament, God took special care to call the people of Israel to live out their faith in community. Christopher J. H. Wright writes, "In the Old Testament God commanded Israel to be a people committed to practical, down-to-earth exercise of compassion and justice, in ways that would reflect and embody God's own commitment to those things."[1] In painstaking detail, God provided instruction for Israel's handling of all aspects of their social life. As a people called by God to be a light to the nations, Israel was to be a charitable, hospitable, and equitable society. And in all these things, the people were to obey God's calling out of a sense of gratitude.

This scriptural foundation is why the church continues to be a missionary people, concerned not only with eternal destinies but also with the present lives and needs of their neighbors. Smith rightly says, "God is Lord not only of the soul but also of the body, the Ruler of not just heaven but also earth. The gospel is good news not just as a rescue plan for embattled souls but as word from the Creator who is redeeming all things."[2] Understanding and embracing these social dimensions of the kingdom of God is a necessary part of life with God.

One concept from the Old Testament that deserves a more regular discussion in Christian circles is the scriptural principle of Jubilee. Appearing among the foundational principles of the Pentateuch is the divine command of a Jubilee year, a piece of legislation designed by God to benefit Israelite society. The following sections of Leviticus 25 are worth reading in full:

> 10 Consecrate the fiftieth year and proclaim a release
> throughout the land to all its inhabitants. It shall be a
> jubilee for you, and each of you shall return to his own
> property, [e]and each of you shall return to his family. 11
> You shall have the fiftieth year as a jubilee; you shall not
> sow, nor harvest its aftergrowth, nor gather grapes from
> its untrimmed vines. 12 For it is a jubilee; it shall be holy
> to you. You shall eat its produce from the field.
>
> 13 On this year of jubilee each of you shall return
> to his own property. 14 Furthermore, if you make a sale

1. Wright, *"Here Are Your Gods,"* 136.
2. Smith, *Imagining the Kingdom*, 154–55.

> to your friend, or buy from your friend's hand, you shall not wrong one another. 15 Corresponding to the number of years after the jubilee, you shall buy from your friend; he is to sell to you according to the number of years of crops. 16 In proportion to a greater number of years you shall increase its price, and in proportion to fewer years you shall decrease its price, because it is the number of crops that he is selling to you. . .
>
> 23 The land, moreover, shall not be sold permanently, because the land is Mine; for you are only strangers and residents with Me. 24 So for every piece of your property, you are to provide for the redemption of the land. . . .
>
> 39 Now if a countryman of yours becomes so poor with regard to you that he sells himself to you, you shall not subject him to a slave's service. 40 He shall be with you as a hired worker, as if he were a foreign resident; he shall serve with you up to the year of jubilee. 41 He shall then leave you, he and his sons with him, and shall go back to his family, so that he may return to the property of his forefathers. 42 For they are My servants whom I brought out from the land of Egypt; they are not to be sold in a slave sale. 43 You shall not rule over him with severity, but are to revere your God. . . .
>
> 54 Even if he is not redeemed by [ag]these means, he shall still leave in the year of jubilee, he and his sons with him. 55 For the sons of Israel are My servants; they are My servants whom I brought out from the land of Egypt. I am the Lord your God. (NASB)

God's mandate provided a generation (fifty years) of opportunity for God's people to work hard to achieve all that they could. And God blessed this sense of ingenuity, innovation, and sharing of space and wealth.

God also wanted to make sure that the fruit of these efforts was not to be generational. Those who had prospered were commanded to lift their brothers and sisters who had fallen into dire circumstances. This was, as Professor Tremper Longman put it in an interview, "a community-oriented kind of approach."[3] Behind this instruction stands the reality that "God owns all things, even the land."

Leviticus 25 teaches that God wanted Israel to reflect his own grace by doing justice and extending mercy to others, a theme that extends throughout the Old Testament prophetic literature. The Jubilee was, in essence, a declaration that any wealth and privilege accumulated were not the sole result of brilliance and effort of people but were directly attributed to the gifts and blessings of God. Conversely, the decisions and actions of others that may have left them in poor health, in prison, devoid of economic or educational opportunities, or some other adverse condition, were not de facto generational curses. God's children were all to experience a kind of reset.

Interestingly, when Jesus commenced his own ministry, he did so by entering his hometown synagogue and announcing his calling in terms of enactment of Jubilee.

> 16 And He came to Nazareth, where He had been brought up; and as was His custom, He entered the synagogue on the Sabbath, and stood up to read. 17 And the scroll of Isaiah the prophet was handed to Him. And He unrolled the scroll and found the place where it was written:
> 18 "The Spirit of the Lord is upon Me,
> Because He anointed Me to bring good news to the poor.
> He has sent Me to proclaim release to captives,
> And recovery of sight to the blind,
> To set free those who are oppressed,
> 19 To proclaim the favorable year of the Lord."
> 20 And He rolled up the scroll, gave it back to the attendant, and sat down; and the eyes of all the people in the synagogue were intently directed at Him. 21 Now He began to say to them, "Today this Scripture has been fulfilled in your hearing." (Luke 4:16–21 NASB)

3. Personal interview with author, 4 August 2021

Drawing explicitly on Isa 61:1–2's reception of Leviticus 25:8–55, Jesus saw his ministry as inaugurating the year of the Lord's favor. A new year of Jubilee had begun.[4] That Jesus announced this new reality at the outset of his ministry indicates how crucial and central it should be to the life of faith. Jesus' proclamation of this theme should not be taken as a sort of timeless principle that is removed from context of redemptive history. Jesus' reference to this pivotal passage in Isaiah (which alludes to Leviticus 25) should be seen as part of his own self-realized eschatological program. His followers remembered Jesus' ministry as the first part of God's ultimate scenario, in which God begins to enact God's kingly rule.[5]

This vision strikes me as applicable and relevant to our own time. As Chris Wright helpfully puts it,

> The moral principles of the jubilee are therefore universalizable on the basis of the moral consistency of God. What God required of Israel in God's land reflects what in principle he desires for humanity on God's earth—namely, broadly equitable distribution of the resources of the earth, especially land, and a curb on the tendency to accumulation with its inevitably oppression and alienation.[6]

That this is a forgotten paradigm in many ways today does not negate the imperative it suggests. Central to Jesus' message is the redistribution of resources, the proper access to which had ceased to keep up with the needs of the moment.

The Jubilee principle acknowledges both the importance of allowing resources to accumulate for a time and the need for a generational reset to ensure that those who have been left out of the current paradigm of prosperity have another chance. And this generational reset occurs regardless of the perceived merit of the recipients. The poor are not assumed to be lazy or helpless. On the contrary, the principle of Jubilee reinforces that the poor are most often the oppressed. Therefore, according to Longman, the Scriptures teach us

4. Sloan, *Favorable Year of the Lord.*
5. Allison, *End of the Ages Has Come.*
6. Wright, *Mission of God*, 296.

that we must work to fight against all systems that create poverty, whether inside or outside the community of faith.[7]

The church lives as a recipient of this Scriptural calling. And our present context should make it clear why it is so pressing, especially as we consider wedding together mission and the creative use of church property. Bethany Hanke Hoang and Kristen Deede Johnson say, "Each movement of the biblical story opens the door to a deeper understanding and invitation to respond to who God is; who God calls his people to be; and the justice, righteousness, and shalom that God longs to see in this world. At each turn in the story, we find God beckoning us further into the justice calling he has placed on our lives."[8]

It's easy to forget how our social situation has changed, which impacts the shape of how we carry out mission. Economists can now offer data to reinforce what we've all witnessed anecdotally: the gap between the ultra-wealthy and the average worker is growing exponentially. Today's rich are much richer, and the hard-working lower and middle classes are barely staying afloat. [9] The events of 2020 revealed these inequalities more clearly than ever before.

Sharing in the resurrection life of Christ necessarily involves service of others. A renewal of the ancient Jubilee acknowledges God's Kingship and gracious rule over all things. True life is found in this posture and set of actions. I believe this is what Jesus meant when he said that he came to give us "life, and that more abundantly" (John 10:10 NIV)

For the church, the most obvious corporate manifestation of Christian witness, this service to others must include use of those real-estate resources, together worth billions of dollars in value, which lay fallow and unused as underutilized and surplus land.

7. Longman, *Bible and the Ballot*, 274.

8. Hoang and Johnson, *Justice Calling*, 6.

9. Piketty, *Capital*.

What if institutions desperate to avoid death are no longer doing what they were meant to do? Does the church become a zombie institution, hoarding resources to keep itself alive, while keeping back those spaces from a world in desperate need of them? Considering Jesus' calling to die to self, we should ask new questions. What if our goal was dying well, or dying honorably? What if we sacrificed old paradigms to new ways of living? What if this was not, in fact, a death but an opportunity to experience new life?

The Jubilee principle of Leviticus 25 explicitly mandates a generational reset of real property. Such a reset ensures that the needs of today are met by the resources held over from yesterday. It frees up the resources for their best and most faithful current use. A culture of hoarding and parsimony begets a world made by those values. A culture of "improvident" generosity begets a world made better by generosity. Is it better for an institution to survive while impoverishing the world, or for an institution to die well, bequeathing to the world that which will bequeath a legacy of hospitality, service, and generosity?

This is one implication, not only of Jesus' appropriation of the Jubilee traditions previously mentioned but of the traditional interpretation of Jesus' teaching in the Parable of the Talents. We can recognize that while we may be stewards of our resources—including church-owned sanctuaries—they are God's. Therefore, they should be used in God's mission to share his love with others.

The Landlord has gone away for a time, but he will return. And when he does, he will expect that those entrusted with these sacred resources will have liberally used them in nurturing the body of Christ growing his kingdom. This is our sacred responsibility.

Many of our struggling churches are still in possession of great wealth and power. Mark DeYmaz says, "God expects church leaders to leverage and wisely steward the assets they've been given in order to generate spiritual, social, and financial ROI. In so doing, churches will bear more fruit than tithes and offerings alone might otherwise yield."[10] We cannot allow our worst, most fear-

10. DeYmaz, *Coming Revolution*, 112.

ful, and miserly impulses to drive our decision-making. There is a larger, greater mandate issued for believers.

What if an embrace of God's Jubilee saturated to a structural level? What if it captured the imagination and vision of religious organizations and churches? Even churches that are currently failing in terms of financial stability and membership can and must succeed in this mission to fulfill God's plan for serving others in our world.

Think of the difference that this mission would make in healing two plagues in our nation: racial injustice and poverty, issues deeply rooted in economic inequality. God's vision of the Jubilee can help us solve many of our most pressing social woes, even as the church fulfills her divinely mandated mission.

If the disciples had not acknowledged Jesus' death on the road to Emmaus, they would never have been able to walk into the new life he had prepared for them. Perhaps our institutions need to say, along with John the Baptist in the Gospel of John (3:30), that Jesus must increase, and we must decrease. Those who will come after us must increase, and we must decrease. Faithful leaders from Moses to Dr. Martin Luther King Jr. blessed the next generation, seeking the good that they themselves would never see in their lifetimes. Our institutions can die well to old ways of being and, in so doing, they can raise up the next generation in new and healthier ways.

Organizations with limited financial paths for sustaining ministry can still be faithful to this vision of Jubilee by embracing new ways of using their existing spaces. Through God's great help and blessing, and with a new awareness of the practical options available, numerous churches and non-profit organizations have already stepped into this revitalized life of faith. For many of these organizations, sacrificing property initially felt like a loss or failure. However, creative uses of otherwise unused church property can both further one's mission and (financially speaking) provide essential lifeblood to an organization.

Faithful allocation of resources to bless the world in Jesus' name makes ministry a joy. Gospel obedience in the form of self-death looks different than a one-time action. Obedience begets faithfulness—a long-term set of practices that cumulatively speak to our love of God and neighbor. That obedience must present the good news in word and deed. The time for change is now, and as the poet June Jordan famously said, "We are the ones we have been waiting for."

In the following chapters, you'll find descriptions of faithful stewards who acted in and with their communities. Nearly across the board, they shared certain characteristics that we should note while reflecting on their stories. As you read, look at how each story demonstrates a need to:

1. Be open-handed
2. Extend God's invitation to all people
3. Care for spoken and unspoken needs simultaneously
4. Work to right wrongs through long-term solutions

This way of driving a church is not typical, let alone typically American. Faithfulness to God's calling doesn't demand more money raised or the preservation of an uninspired calling. Real, lasting care involves solving immediate problems, reversing systemic injustices, and extending God's love. Today is the time to act. "This is the day the LORD has made; we will rejoice and be glad in it" (Ps 118:24 NKJV).

Every church—dying or otherwise—is called to a lifelong process of following God to offer untapped church resources for the greater good. Evaluating your church's health is the first step in this journey. Accurately assessing your congregation's strengths and weaknesses will allow you to make effectual plans for your church's future. Consider each of these statements, answering yes or no.

Church Health Assessment

1. Your church has clear mission and vision statements.
2. Your mission and vision statements are supported by church leadership and often emphasized to members.
3. Your church's mission defines and guides each ministry and program.
4. Your church's mission and vision inform the core values of your church.
5. Your church's mission takes precedence over church policies and procedures.
6. You have the right leadership team to grow your church in accordance with its mission and vision.
7. Ministry and church leaders have clear, defined roles, goals, and expectations.
8. Current volunteers and facilities are adequate to see progress in your mission, vision, and goals.
9. Overall, your members live peaceably with each other.
10. Most of your members are not retired.
11. Your church reflects the demographics of your local community.
12. Giving has remained consistent or grown throughout the last year.
13. Budget concerns are not the sole determining factor in pursuing a new ministry or opportunity.
14. Your church's morale could be described as joyous.
15. Your church's culture is diverse and dynamic.
16. You can identify three to five ways your church has grown over the last twelve months.
17. You can identify three to five areas of growth that you plan to address over the next twelve months.
18. You can show how your leadership, volunteers, and members are pursuing God.

19. Mentorship among members is supported and encouraged.
20. Volunteers are trained, encouraged, and empowered to do their work well.
21. Your church contributes to the financial literacy of its members.
22. Church leaders are engaged and active in the community.
23. You can identify one to three areas of need in your local community that your church regularly aims to meet.
24. Your church strives to make a difference in your local community through concrete initiatives and relevant ministries.
25. Your church regularly works in harmony with other churches to accomplish a common goal.

How is your church doing?

Healthy	Monitor	Review	Concern	Critical
You answered "no" for fewer than 5 questions	You answered "no" for 5–10 questions	You answered "no" for 11–15 questions	You answered "no" for 16–20 questions	You answered "no" for more than 21 questions

If you've studied the results of the assessment and determined that your congregation is ready to have this conversation, it's time to consider three options: merging, leasing, or selling. In this book, I will break down what each of these options entails, covering both real-world logistics and spiritual implications. I also offer stories of churches that have attempted one or more of these options to varying degrees of success.

I hope these chapters serve as both a challenge and a source of encouragement. If you can follow God's call into a more imaginative use of physical space and real-estate property, your work will never be in vain. My prayer is that every struggling church can embrace these ideas for the advancement of God's purposes.

3

So That Our Joy May Be Made Complete

Eventually, all things merge into one,
and a river runs through it.

—Norman McLean

In the corporate world, businesspeople love using buzzwords that set them apart as competent experts. If you want a real-time look at the insider-speak of corporate culture, visit a coffee shop in a business district around 7 AM. You'll hear people intensely discussing "onboarding," "synergy," "bandwidth," "alignment," "hyperlocal," and a whole host of other terms. While buzzwords speak to many facets of a larger operation, behind them all is an understanding that long-term business goals are about growth. And these days, sustainability (buzzword!) is considered a team effort. Conceptualizing and capitalizing on long-term teamwork is a hallmark of many early twenty-first-century business models.[1]

1. Edmondson, *Teaming.*

The value of teamwork is one of the reasons that large companies choose to join forces through mergers. Growing a team and a customer base can lead to large financial successes, and combining two of these enterprises could be market-changing: Exxon and Mobil, Walt Disney and Pixar, AT&T and Time Warner, Google and Android. The list goes on and on. Mergers are one of the most effective ways a company can gain momentum in their market.

Building on these principles, mergers are also available to churches. Sometimes, long-term ministry success can occur only if more leadership is provided, if more people are on board, or if more financial support is provided. But merging churches is not for the faint of heart. Like any marriage, church mergers require careful consideration of all potential risks and rewards.

While often the first option struggling church leaders consider, mergers aren't a magical fix. A church's death offers a glimpse at how Christ is pushing us towards is new work; to save that church might cut short the progress that could, or should, be made. Too often, a dying church hopes the life of the other will reinvigorate it, that this transfusion will cure the illness creeping in. Often, however, these desperation mergers provide only a brief relief, with the systemic problems never being addressed and death and decay being kept at bay only temporarily.

Ultimately, mergers can mask a refusal to truly die to failing ways of doing ministry.

In their seminal book *Better Together*, Jim Tomberlin and Warren Bird, arguably the two leading experts on church mergers in North America, suggest that there are at least five reasons that churches must *not* consider a merger: preservation, maintaining the status quo, a one-sided retirement plan, steeple-jacking, or denominational pressure. Rather, they say, "healthy mergers work best when they're birthed from healthy motives. Shady means are never a wise path to a God-honoring end."[2]

Leaders must stay attuned to this dynamic when considering motivations and pressures in the hearts and minds of their congregants, especially when the possibility of a merger arises. People

2. Tomberlin and Bird, *Better Together*, 31.

will gravitate towards self-preservation. Memories are wed to visualized spaces and places. So even before conversations about any future possibilities to merge take place, a congregation must be led to re-envision their story through the lens of God's story, a redemptive mission that requires us to hold even our dearest memories loosely. We must help people realize that we are meant to make disciples and cherish people, not make buildings and cherish our spaces.

As we evaluate congregational health, it is important to continually take the temperature of the congregation to see how deeply discipleship is intersecting with conversations about missional merging. Here are some helpful questions:

- As you talk to leaders and congregants, do you sense a willingness to die to previous ways of doing ministry?
- Are your leaders and congregants on board with a vision of serving the community in a new way?
- As you talk about completely giving yourselves over to a new thing, is there a spirit of oneness and surrender?

❧

As you consider a merger, Tomberlin and Bird helpfully delineate a Scriptural vision for this process: "The combining, integrating, and unifying of people, structures, systems, and resources to achieve a common purpose: doing life and ministry together as a vibrant, healthy, local expression of Christ's body, the church."[3] Too often we are failing to be the church. Any merger that occurs should be done considering Christ's larger command to go out into our communities.

"Is there a biblical justification for church mergers?" Tomberlin and Bird ask. Their answer is spot on: while *merger* is not used explicitly in the New Testament, words like *graft*, *reconcile*, *unite*,

3. Tomberlin and Bird, *Better Together*, 3.

and *marry* are.[4] When discussing these passages, Tomberlin and Bird summarize the grand impetus: in mergers, God is doing a new thing (Isa 43:19), thus helping people reach new levels of unity, maturity, and fullness in Christ (Eph 4:13). Additionally, Tomberlin and Bird point out that the New Testament speaks of all nations coming to God's temple, which is a house of prayer (Mark 11:17), and the book of Acts, followed by Paul's letters, puts significant emphasis on Christ-following gentiles and Jews coming together in Christ (Col 3:11; Eph 2:15–16). The idea of coming together to accomplish more for the kingdom of God is one embedded throughout the Bible. However, the logistics remain unclear.

In the most successful mergers, there is typically a lead church and a joining church. Tomberlin and Bird describe how a lead church will determine the dominant culture, and the joining church conforms to that model. These roles aren't usually decided by who has the most space, membership, or budget.

Which church should serve as lead is determined by "the state of health and forward momentum." They go on: "A large but mostly empty facility can be more of a liability than an asset if the congregation is small and declining in size." Congregations and their leadership must decide which church should consider leading and which should follow, and parties must agree on a central mission. Establishing these roles and embracing a biblical model for merging is just the beginning.

Tomberlin and Bird present three types of viable church mergers.

First is the rebirth model. In this case, a joining church realizes their inability to continue as a congregation. Due to this, they surrender across the board. Tomberlin and Bird suggest that the most successful rebirths occur in this situation. A joining church decides to "relinquish everything to the lead church—its name, facilities, staff, ministries, and glorious path—all in exchange for

4. Tomberlin and Bird, *Better Together*, 10.

a second life."[5] This demonstrates a commitment to death and rebirth in whatever way God leads. In such a situation, a lead church must take special care to account for this surrender and to willingly "incorporate [the joining church] into the new identity."

Tomberlin and Bird also discuss the adoption model. This is not for a church in its final death throes but for "stable or stuck churches" that need new synergy as they seek to anticipate and prevent a decline. Adopted churches bring together their people, finances, and facilities for long-term renewed energy. But as these churches don't often have the same understanding of their own mortality, congregations are more likely to view the merger as a mistake if (and when) conflict occurs.

A final, somewhat similar merger is that of a marriage model. This is "when two comparable churches, similar in size and/or health, realign with each other under a united vision and new leadership configuration."[6] Tomberlin and Bird suggest that the reason that such a merger works is because of shared missional values. However, shared pastoral roles can present a challenge. Additionally, in such a situation, who is to lead and who is to follow?

There's not always a clear path to solving your church's decline, a clear model that you should consider and embrace. It takes prayerful divine wisdom to navigate solutions, but having thoughtful, intentional conversations is essential to your church's hope. As you consider which merging model may be right for your church, here are five essential questions you and your council must address.

Does it make missional sense?

If a new merger will not make you more focused on mission, it's an easy no. Likewise, if a congregation feels called to serve a neighborhood or larger demographic, but a merger possibility doesn't

5. Tomberlin and Bird, *Better Together*, 66.

6. Tomberlin and Bird, *Better Together*, 71.

allow for the fulfillment of that calling, that merger should not be pursued.

Does the merger allow for better use of facilities and finances?

If a merger creates more unused space, alarms should go off. The vision of a merger must create solutions to the problems that led to the need for a merger. Likewise, while financial problems may not be solved outright by merging, it is pertinent to think about how money is geared towards external, ministries of mercy.

Do the congregations mesh as people?

Every congregation is full of different personalities. While some describe the potential merger process as something like a courtship, we must urge our people to be themselves and to freely reveal not only their strengths but also their weaknesses. It takes time to consider a merger. People need to get to know one another. Leaders need to discern strengths and weaknesses and to openly discuss them and pray about them.

Do the congregational cultures clash?

Just as each church is full of different people, churches do things differently. Some celebrate the sacrament of communion weekly; others celebrate it monthly. Some pastors take a yearly extended vacation to recharge; other pastors wait for several years before taking a much longer sabbatical. Preaching content, style, and length, as well as musical styles, contribute to church culture, too. Any new merger respects each congregation's storied history, even when uniting around a new future together.

Do the leadership and congregation sense the Spirit's clear leading to the merger?

Without a widespread sense of divine propulsion forward, there are too many problems to go forward with a merger. Individual and corporate prayer are part of process. Hearing from the Spirit is not just a step, but the most foundational aspect of considering whether to proceed with a merger.

Congregations considering a merger not only have to wrestle with how they fit together in terms of people and mission but also property. A good broker can help churches sort through property issues. Three central issues need to be addressed as merging congregations consider which building might be the new home:

- *Location* (both the physical churches and the communities that they serve)
- *Property condition* (keeping in mind both short term issues—routine repairs and deferred maintenance—and long-term challenges—remainder of a mortgage, long-term facility needs, and the possibility of churches losing their tax-exempt status in the future)
- *Aesthetics* (does either church structure better embody the church's ethos?)

2020 was perhaps the most difficult year in the average living American's experience. Amid ongoing vitriol and community breakdowns, the local church still has a chance to model what God's future can and will look like. How incredible would it be for the public witness of the church if local bodies that shouldn't fit together (humanly speaking) merge and do good for others? Jesus' prayer for unity in the Garden of Gethsemane applies: "I am not asking on behalf of these alone, but also for those who believe in Me through their word, that they may all be one; just as You, Father, are in Me and I in You, that they also may be in Us, so that the world may believe that You sent Me. The glory which You have given Me I also have given to them, so that they may be one, just as We are one" (John 17:20–22 NASB).

One of the great wins of merging can be selling excess space to benefit both the church and the community. For instance, a nonprofit organization might gain the underutilized space resulting in new community outreaches, even as a newly merged congregation has an influx of funds to hire a new pastor that focuses on outward-facing related ministries.

Unfortunately, a real obstacle that stands in the way of such a scenario is the theological commitments of individual churches. Congregations can become so focused on denominational and theological distinctives that they lose sight of the one true gospel.

In a recent conversation with a pastor in California who was overseeing a thriving church plant, he recounted how his church had grown to nearly 250 people, only to discover that they were stuck in a tight space, with limited options for growth. When I suggested my friend consider a church merger, he balked at the idea.

The problems, he suggested, were denominational differences and legal boundaries around some denominations sharing spaces with other churches. This pastor would rather pursue the lease of a commercial building rather than go through the hassle of navigating theological and legal issues. For him, it didn't make sense to expend energy on all the bureaucracy.

This is an unfortunate reality. In an era when the church should be unified in sharing a message of hope to the world, we sequester ourselves into ever smaller camps that value what's familiar and easy over what's active and effective. This is a failure by all accounts.

If we wish to move forward as a church, repentance must be pursued. As Karl Barth reminds us, that opportunity is a gift, a "chance to come back home to the place which God prepared for us."[7] Only then can we see the beauty of the gospel's power fully unveiled before us and the watching world. In this posture,

7. Barth, *Deliverance*, 72.

we can overcome even the most obstinate denominational and theological hurdles. Bandy and Brooks say it best: "God's vision is bursting denominational inwardness and expanding ecumenical expectations."[8]

❧

So which approach to merging provides the clearest pathway for success? That is determined by which model can best address the inevitable hurdles in this process. The most fundamental challenge with any merger is the question of who will accept the role of the subservient partner, the joining church. It is a challenging task and explains why many of these mergers fail. When the question of a merger arises, and with it the discomfort of knowing there will be upheaval to all the habits, practices, and processes that have become integrally woven into the very fabric of each congregation, a perfect equilibrium between the desires and needs of both churches is impossible to achieve.

The only way to true success is that one of the churches must elect to become completely subservient to the other, best seen in the rebirth model. This needs to be discussed openly, honestly, and transparently within the context of any merger discussion. To not do so is to sow the seeds of discord and disillusion for the future. Miscommunication and ill-founded expectations lead to feelings of betrayal as one of the churches feels like they have lost control over the future of the church. This explains why in many cases a merged church is more like a corporate takeover, with the historic pastors, staff, and many of the congregation leaving to either find a new church with which to worship or leaving the faith altogether.

But it doesn't have to be this way.

The truth is that the decision to become subservient is akin to accepting the Christian belief that new life can only be found in death. That only by releasing control to the other church and truly becoming a servant to the other can the new life of the merged

8. Bandy and Brooks, *Church Mergers*, 7.

congregation succeed. And despite a culture that says that becoming subservient is being less and that we should instead adopt the strategies to wrest power from the other, the Way, the Truth and the Life is found in the example of Jesus' death on the cross. We must embrace the cup as Jesus did.

Despite living in a world that tries to convince us to avoid challenges, the way of Christ is to embrace all seasons. A season in which our church is dying is a grace-filled opportunity to drink the cup that Jesus did and, in doing so, embrace new life. On this subject, Henri Nouwen writes: "Sin and death entrap us. Drinking the cup, as Jesus did, is the way out of that trap. It is the way to salvation. It is a hard way, a painful way, a way we want to avoid at all costs. Often it even seems an impossible way. Still, unless we are willing to drink our cup, real freedom will elude us. This is not only the freedom that comes after we have completely emptied our cup—that is, after we have died. No, this freedom comes to us every time we drink from the cup of life, whether a little or much."[9]

Perhaps this is the wisdom that all churches must come to embrace if we are to overcome the challenges of a culture that seems to reject much of our Christian message. By embracing all the seasons of life—even those that call us to become subservient to others as the only certain path of new life—we can become active participants in God's loving plan. "To everything there is a season, and a time for every purpose under heaven: A time to be born, and a time to die; a time to plant, and a time to pluck up that which is planted" (Eccl 3:1–2 NKJV).

9. Nouwen, *Can You Drink*, 96.

4

Parables on Merging

We must adjust to changing times
and still hold to unchanging principles.

—President Jimmy Carter

Our attitudes and interactions may have changed over the years, but the Western church at large remains functionally segregated. The apostle Paul teaches us that "there is neither Jew nor Greek, there is neither slave nor free, there is neither male nor female; for you are all one in Christ Jesus" (Gal 3:28 NKJV). But American Christians have long been blind to the glorious diversity of God's kingdom.

Fortunately, some are realizing that diversity is indeed beautiful and one of the marks of a church that truly reflects its entire community. Besides intentionally working together on projects and outreach, some church bodies have gone so far as to say, "We can do more together than we ever could apart." A merger between racially diverse communities is one important way that we see the kingdom of God taking shape in our Western context today.

Fortunately, I've seen churches actively and successfully work towards those ends, especially in the process of considering and enacting a merger with another body of Christ.

The Story of Pilgrim Congregational Church

Pastor Raymond Trembath arrived in the northeastern section of Oakland, California, in the early 1980s to take on a pastoral role at Pilgrim Congregational Church. Pilgrim was in the process of forming an identity as a congregationally led church independent of their denomination. Pilgrim's leadership was at peace with this decision and ready to move forward. As the second millennium rapidly approached its end, Pastor Raymond was excited about how God might be leading the congregation to face a new season of growth.

Like so many pastors of community churches, Pastor Raymond met people in the neighborhood. With over five hundred homes within walking distance, opportunity for ministry literally surrounded Pilgrim. But knocking on doors to invite people to church wasn't the best way to make connections in this community because, as Pastor Raymond realized, he was an outsider, ethnically speaking. The majority demographic of the neighborhood was no longer white as Central East Oakland had swung from just over 90 percent Caucasian to almost 90 percent African American in a relatively short time. And despite this shift, Pastor Raymond's congregation remained entirely white. As time passed, Pilgrim lost members to death and relocation, with very few of their neighbors ever visiting the white island of churchgoers.

Before long, Pilgrim was officially "people poor, but facilities rich." In prayer and discussion with the remaining leaders, Pastor Trembath realized that the church needed to think creatively about using its space to serve a community that wasn't interested in attending his church.

Pilgrim's leadership formulated a goal. They would seek to provide space to a primarily African American- or Pacific Islander-led church that might better serve the community. Perhaps a familiar face might lead to greater missional impact. An African American church began renting out Pilgrim's fellowship hall. Pastor Raymond developed a close friendship with their pastor, Gary. As the pastors became friends, the possibility of a merger naturally arose. Pastor Raymond had caught a vision of the importance of bridging the gap with his neighbors. For ministry to work, the fullness of God's people needed to be present in the neighborhood church. Could Pilgrim merge seamlessly with her sister church and move together into a new, revitalized future?

Pastor Gary and Pastor Raymond believed a merger was the way forward, but they had not yet developed a formal process of consideration. There was no sit-down between lay leaders to consider potential pitfalls. Despite this oversight, they grew excited about their renewed kingdom vision of what could happen if a truly inclusive community were formed through a merger. This discussion was entirely driven by best serving the immediate community, not the congregation: Pastor Raymond wanted to use Pilgrim's property well and partner with another church that better reflected the neighborhood.

As word of the idea spread within each congregation, both groups appreciated the pastors' unity of purpose. They decided to spend four weeks together in a blended worship service. Despite being open to the merger, however, many congregants left feeling dismayed and displaced after the month's trial.

Years later, Pastor Raymond reflected on the experience. "At the end of four weeks, everyone hated everybody. It was not that anyone was wrong, but the worship style was wrong for both churches. Our services were an hour in length; their services were two hours. My sermons tended to be 30 minutes. His sermons tended to be 60 minutes. They had drums, and we had an organ. To our credit, we did this for four weeks. We then realized that no one was happy, so we went back to meeting separately. I would never say it was wrong; it was just that our worship styles and services didn't align. How God handles that in heaven is his business. For us, it just didn't work out."

Fortunately, despite this shared understanding that God was not leading the two churches to become one, they maintained a spirit of unity in mission. For years, Pilgrim rented out their facilities at below-market rates and joined their sister church in community mission projects and outreach events. Outreach was a partial success in terms of Pilgrim's public witness. People in the surrounding community noticed that black and white Christians were working alongside each other in common mission. Despite the failed merger, Pilgrim gained a renewed mission and a firm sense that they must not cling to their facilities.

Could the failed merger have been prevented? Despite having honorable intentions, Pastors Raymond and Pastor Gary never identified or addressed their fundamental differences ahead of time. For these churches, discerning God's will involved worshipping for a season, but further clarity could have been achieved through a formal comparison of church worship services. There's never a competition between our discernment process and the Spirit's work in our hearts and minds. As the Spirit works with us, we must cultivate discernment through difficult conversations and considerations.

Pilgrim Congregational Church: Appraisals and Contingencies

- Pursue relationships with other congregations organically.
- Find a church with similar vision and missional impulse.
- Stay open to experimenting outside worship comfort zones.
- Take time to consider insurmountable differences.
- Move in a new direction if something is not working.

The Story of Morning Star and Grace Churches

Pastor Josh Wroten founded Morning Star Church in 2002. Cecil, Pastor Wroten's wife (who is Filipina by birth), actively served alongside him in the Asian-American community. In a spectacular season of ministry, people who had never seen the interior of a church building were baptized and discipled under Pastor Wroten's leadership. In a decade, over a hundred people were baptized and became involved in the life of the growing church plant.

Morning Star Church was in the minority of Protestant churches in the early 2000s because it was small yet growing. Like other church plants, they encountered a problem in finding enough space to worship together.

Pastor Wroten, who is an advocate of right-size churches, was not interested in growing numbers to fit a massive building somewhere, but in continuing to equip the church for God's mission. His goal for locating a church facility was, appropriately, positioned between sustainability and his ministry's own long-term work of evangelism and discipleship.

Morning Star first met in a rented hotel conference room, then in a public school, and finally in a former school district site that the district had taken out of operation as a surplus property. That latter space worked for an extended season, with the church continuing to go about the work of ministry. Then, something unexpected happened.

The school district made the decision to sell the surplus property. Morning Star would need to find a home. The larger Bay Area, where Morning Star was located, is notorious for high costs of leasing and/or purchasing space. As Pastor Wroten and the congregation looked for a new space, the idea of a temporary facility was difficult to fathom. It took tremendous energy each week to set up and take down a site. But signing a long-term lease at a fixed location brought its own set of challenges. To absorb the cost of such an arrangement, Morning Star would have to compromise their mission by tying themselves to financial obligations. As the deadline approached, a friend reached out to Pastor Wroten, asking, "Why don't you consider merging with Grace Church?"

In recent years, this congregation had been two separate churches: Bethel Baptist and Cornerstone Christian. They had merged into Grace Church, but the merger had not gone well. Staff, vision, and theological conflicts plagued the process. In the lead-up to the merger, due diligence had not been done to assess each church's position and needs, and a lack of communication and transparency dictated decision-making. Additionally, one essential staff member, who many believed would become the new lead pastor, resigned. The newly formed Grace Church was experiencing a period of decline. They lost almost half their congregation in less than four years. Morale was down, and new people weren't visiting.

To their credit, the leaders of Grace Church responded to the crisis by inviting in a church assessment team led by none other than Pastor Wroten. Since receiving the recommendation three years earlier, Grace Church had been working hard to create change, but the church was still in need of new leadership to implement their renewed vision. Pastor Wroten listened to his friend's suggestion and decided to interview for the open position as senior pastor of Grace with the intention of bringing his congregation along.

During this period of discernment, Morning Star's lease was approaching its termination date. As affirmations continued to come for his candidacy at Grace Church, Pastor Wroten came to realize that the only way forward was, in faith, to close Morning Star. Since Grace Church had been through too much in their past merger to do it again, Pastor Wroten came up with a creative solution: why not lead his former congregation to Grace Church and to ask both congregations to re-enter a formal membership process?

Painstakingly, Pastor Wroten began to let go of his long-beloved church plant. In a series of dessert conversations and small group gatherings, Pastor Wroten charted out his vision for a future with Grace Church. "We tried to be very up-front and open-handed," he recalls. "We knew Morning Star would have to die for this to work. We couldn't go in and take it over."

Fortunately, the lay leadership at Grace owned the transition and led their people to overwhelmingly call Pastor Wroten, with full endorsement of his plan. The merger—that wasn't really a merger (on paper)—was a success.

Apart from Pastor Wroten, the leadership at Morning Star stepped down from their positions. Pastor Wroten came to the (new) Grace Church with the open-handed posture that he had embodied in the lead up to the transition. He met with congregants at Grace, shepherded them, and helped them see their risk was worth it. Both partners entered the relationship invested for the long haul. Such humble faithfulness must be present for any long-term partnership to work. By the grace of God, it is possible.

Pastor Wroten freely admits that this success story was God's gift. The attitude that prevailed among leadership and congregants was one of reliance on God to make the new church a healthy vessel. Even then, with conversation, transparency, and good leadership, there were difficulties. Tensions could be felt between various members as dress, race, and worship practices differed. Neither church was the same as it had been in the past. The merger birthed an entirely new thing.

After an initial period of "family blending," as Pastor Wroten calls it, renewed, outward-facing mission became the new normal. New faces began to appear. Grace Church transitioned from being a majority Asian-American church—with an Asian-American culture and ethos—to a multi-ethnic church with no ethnic majority and much more diversity. The new church was more successful because of what the congregation was able to do together.

Bandy and Page describe the central role that pastors play in a successful church merger.

> The credibility comes from the depth and discipline of spiritual life, and the transparency of the leader to reveal Jesus Christ. The courage comes from the readiness of the leader (and his or her family) to stake life and lifestyle on achieving God's purpose over institutional survival.

> Innovation must always trump tradition, even as tradition must always inform innovations. The credibility of the leader to balance innovation and tradition is important. But the courage of the leader to prioritize innovation *over* tradition is crucial.[1]

Pastors must embody the peaceful, fruitful, relational approach that they want to see conveyed.

In addition to Pastor Wroten's good leadership, others had to actively cooperate with him. The congregations had to work with each other fully and intentionally, even in the discernment process. This attests to developing maturity. Such maturity must be central to the life of any church that wishes to flourish.

Morning Star and Grace Church: Appraisals and Contingencies

- Stay focused on missional growth not numbers.
- Work with wise counsel to consider creative solutions.
- Develop accountability and trust with all parties.
- Let go of good plans to embrace the better plan.
- Approach leadership with humility and respect for other people's ideas.
- Even in the face of challenges, remain deliberate and transparent in messaging.

The Story of Niles Discovery Church

Scripture is full of agricultural metaphors. As noted earlier, one of particular interest for me is that of believers as fruit, attached to Jesus, the vine. Relational connection to Jesus is foundational for the work of any church leader. This life-giving, beautiful engagement

1. Bandy and Brooks, *Church Mergers*, 14.

can't be replaced by any amount of careful planning, teamwork, or larger networking.

In Matthew 13, we learn about a field in which a farmer scatters seed. The seed, according to Jesus, falls on different types of soil. Depending on the condition of the soil, the seed either does or does not grow. As churches go about their work today, leaders never fully know whether the seed they scatter will bear gospel fruit. But this knowledge doesn't stop the work; it is part of the reality of working in God's spiritual economy.

Looking at things from a long view, we can see that our work and God's aren't at odds, when done with the right motives. Mergers can greatly advance the gospel when they allow church leaders to focus on outreach, a key facet of discipleship.

Pastor Jeff Spencer was wrapping up his second decade in pastoral ministry when he became the senior pastor of Niles Congregational Church, a congregation in the United Church of Christ. The congregation was older but vibrant. Community outreach and mission had always been part of Niles Congregational's DNA. In fact, Pastor Spencer quickly realized that the yearly budget was usually outspent due to a desire to try out new and more innovative ways of being Christ's people for the community.

During his first year at Niles, Pastor Spencer developed a friendship with Pastor Joe at First Christian Church of Fremont, a Disciples of Christ congregation. First Christian was financially stable due to a building sale and relocation, but their attendance was dwindling.

Even though neither First Christian nor Niles Congregational was in danger of immediately dying, Pastor Jeff and Pastor Joe realized that if their churches joined forces, they might grow. More importantly, bringing both churches together through a formal merge could allow them to accomplish bigger things in the community than either could do alone. Both pastors understood the need for congregational compatibility, and they knew it would take time and intentional efforts to make a merger work.

As the financial crisis of 2008 struck, First Christian and Niles Congregational formally explored the possibility of merging.

Looking back, Pastor Jeff saw this as a time to invite people slowly but surely into a reimagining of Niles' future. Because openness was gently encouraged from the top, people were able to process the possibilities and fears of loss that would inevitably come. As the congregations formed committees, trust developed between congregants and leadership teams. Without this slowly unfolding process and the trust that it engendered, Niles and First Christian would probably not have had the will to proceed.

A key part of the process became a period of looking at each church's self-perceived identity. Through a series of workshops, lay leaders and staff from each church took intentional steps to identify their own church's demographics, theological commitments and values, ways of doing ministry, and internal dynamics. This effort paid off huge dividends.

When each congregation revealed their answers to these fundamental identity questions, it became clear that Niles and First Christian were in lockstep. Despite some differences in how finances were handled, the overall polity, ministry, and social norms of each church were deeply in sync. One of the fascinating, unique, and beautiful aspects of Niles Discovery's story is that they managed to stay simultaneously a part of two denominations at the same time. In their case, the bylaws of both previous congregations and their respective denominations allowed for a church to simultaneously be fully part of two complementary denominations.

Even after the merger vote was overwhelmingly passed in both congregations, several members at Niles Congregational were troubled at the decision to relocate to First Christian's facilities. Even though it was larger, Niles Congregational would leave her historic home. Pastor Jeff knew that Niles Congregational was making a good decision to merge, but that didn't lessen the pain and grief, especially to those who spent decades worshiping in the historic building of Niles Congregational, including one member in her fifties who had been part of the church for her entire life. Many weddings had been celebrated there. Parents had their children baptized and confirmed in the church, raising them in the children's programs and classes.

As the preparation for the sale of the historic property got underway, members came to Pastor Jeff and said things like, "That is the pew where I mourned my father's death" or "This is the place where I found support as I went through my divorce." There were a lot of spiritual and personal memories attached to the facility, and each of these had to be acknowledged and released with trust in God's bigger plans.

Pastor Jeff met the pained conversations and tears with a knowledge that his people were not intentionally standing in the way; they were mourning. Their shared loss of sacred space had to be re-conceptualized. "I didn't see it as being a contrarian for the sake of being a contrarian," Pastor Jeff said. "Talking about the fact that all who had a connection to that building would grieve helped. . . . But you can't fix grief; you can only go through it."

Niles Congregational and First Christian decided that coming together as one church would involve mutual, sacrificial concern for the other congregation. This required careful planning and shared input about the future shape of the new congregation's life. Each church's previous ways of doing committees were scrapped. New names for each congregational committee were taken on. By creating this new language for shared church responsibilities, a tone was set early on that Niles Congregational, the larger of the two congregations, was not interested in taking over.

With this sense of a shared future as one congregation, they chose a new name: Niles Discovery Church. With the synergy of these movements, new faces began to appear within the community. Projects took on innovative, creative shape, and they were then reinvented during the COVID-19 outbreak. Niles Discovery was poised and ready to act as God led.

The journey of these two congregations is a beautiful picture of the promises and perils of mergers. Both congregations had the blessing of skilled, seasoned pastors that knew how important it was to fully invest themselves in the success of the other congregation. Taking on new committee titles and a new church name demonstrated the solidarity and a commitment to creating something together.

Niles Congregational Church: Appraisals and Contingencies

- Be intentional about timely decision-making.
- Define identity with input from all parties involved.
- Carefully consider the emotional impact of leaving behind storied spaces.
- Model communal grief and leave space for mourning the loss of space.
- Approach the merger sacrificially and with open arms for the other congregation.
- Hold onto old ways loosely to make way for true, innovative partnership.

5

With Glad and Sincere Hearts

If we have no peace, it is because we have forgotten that we belong to each other.

—Mother Teresa

When church leaders first begin to wonder about how they might get more value out of their property, typically the first question they consider is "Can we lease out some space?" It's worth considering as an option. But before we get into the details of *how* to lease church property, first let me explain exactly what is often meant by *lease*.

Leasing allows someone else to use your property under defined terms, but the property remains yours. One party provides the property; the other party provides something in exchange. However, exactly what is given in exchange can vary widely and should be considered carefully by the property-holding party, especially if that party is a church.

As with all endeavors that involve stewardship of church resources, money should not be the only or even the primary motivator in this decision. Faithful use of church property to advance the work of the gospel is the calling of the church. Leasing out property to the highest bidder suggests a lack of mission alignment. Likewise, squeezing a lessee for all they're worth is missionally problematic and unethical. Unused space is also a problem. There is no possibility of positive mission effect when no one benefits from an unused space for the bulk of a week.

James's words about hoarded wealth apply:

> Anyone, then, who knows the right thing to do and fails to do it, commits sin. Come now, you rich people, weep and wail for the miseries that are coming to you. Your [hoarded] riches have rotted. . . . Your gold and silver have rusted, and their rust will be evidence against you. (4:17—5:2 NRSV)

Leasing a portion of church property can have indirect benefits that church leaders may not anticipate. An indirect benefit is any good thing that results from the lease for which the church that owns the property is not the primary beneficiary, and understanding how churches can help their communities through leasing involves a change of perception.

Congregations must die to any sense of personal ownership. Part of letting go of our future hopes and plans involves trusting God with the present—especially as it includes our material sources of wealth. Our spaces belong to God, and we are stewards or account managers for a time. When we buy in to this perspective, our focus moves from "how do we guard this space?" to "how can we make this space available and accessible to those who need it most?"

This means that before a church thinks about how to monetize an underutilized space through leasing, leaders should consider how that space may benefit others. Of course, sharing a space may increase the cost of upkeep and maintenance. It's reasonable for a church to charge a nominal rent to cover these expenses, especially for congregations with already tight budget restraints. But when money derived from leasing is the first concern in a discussion about using church space, a larger problem of priorities exists.

The good news about ensuring positive indirect effects of a lease agreement is that there is no shortage of those who need space. The task of learning who might benefit from using a church's facilities can often be solved by asking. Most churches are surrounded by organizations that sufficiently align with their overall mission, and it is up to the church to make itself available.

If you generously share space, your abundance can and will benefit your community. It's that simple. Has God given you a space that you can't fully use? Yes. And God has also given you neighbors and neighborhood organizations that can.

❧

Direct effects of leasing are those that primarily benefit your church. Admittedly, this is the category that is often first in mind when churches consider leasing. Direct benefits might include increased revenue, increased traffic in the building leading to an increase in attendance or membership, an increased profile in the community, and a boost to the reputation of the church. Honestly, I hope that as you read this list you see that it is full of alarm bells.

It is rare that a lease agreement makes a big enough dent in a church's finances to offset real systemic financial problems related to demographic decline, reduced giving, or mission creep. Leasing will not solve all your problems. Further, the other elements of this list are never guaranteed—you can't write them into a lease agreement or demand them as proof of a worthwhile venture. If these are the direct benefits you hope to gain from a lease, you aren't being realistic.

In a short blog piece entitled "Why We Don't Rent Out Space," Christian Reformed Church pastor Sam Hamstra discusses leasing to other congregations. Hamstra asserts that Christ would think such a rental arrangement would be "bizarre" or "strange."

As his thinking unfolds, Hamstra softens his position—a little. He admits that there might *appear* to be benefits to a church leasing space to another group. For example, the leasing church, which he calls the "landlord," gets revenue to maintain their space and the tenant receives the "benefit of space designed for religious purposes." On the surface the arrangement appears ethical. But Hamstra believes that Jesus would still oppose such a landlord-tenant relationship as "inconsistent with the fruit of his work of reconciliation."

Hamstra almost goes so far as to suggest that kingdom work between churches ought to take place entirely apart from financial interactions. As a counterexample to renting out space, Hamstra showcases a CRC congregation that freely shares space with a younger congregation. Interestingly, Hamstra admits that the sharing congregation in this case didn't need the money. That is a key admission, I think, as to how Hamstra understands who best can lease out space. But what about the rest of the country's churches that are not so financially secure? Hamstra polemicizes against the use of contractual and financial arrangements, even for the sake of ministry survival. Here's his final summary statement: "Clearly, then, money—not the advancement of the kingdom of God—often determines whether or not a congregation shares space with another congregation. And, as a wise person once taught me, when money is the primary basis for a decision, it will be the wrong decision."

As I've reflected on Hamstra's perspective, I am moved by the faith of my brother and the sister church he mentions. I truly appreciate that he has thought about church property and wants to use it well. But I believe Hamstra's case is somewhat overstated. Kingdom partnerships do not have to be taken on irrespective of financial transactions and legal agreements. They could, of course, and the book of Acts paints an ideal situation of believers sharing all things in common (2:44). While we can fully embrace that that we must act in accordance with this principle whenever possible, the kingdom needs generous financial backing to play a part in the present age. The means by which God grows his kingdom is through the instrument of human agency. It's the primary way God has chosen to work in the world.

God owns the cattle on a thousand hills (Ps 50:12) and asks us to treat "our" property and possessions accordingly. We are commanded to live out of faith, and the Spirit empowers us to do just that, day by day. In the end, we can look back on any achievement and say, "not I, but Christ in me!"

We can appreciate that Hamstra doesn't want to see churches maximize financial success through squeezing every dollar they can out of a ministry leasing their space. In this way, Hamstra's work is a challenging reminder. We must always take care to highlight kingdom teachings about not loving wealth, nor mistreating others that are less advantaged. In fact, we are indeed called to radical generosity. This form of hospitality is an extension of God's grace-filled economy. We must not fall prey to the path of the enemy. We all face the danger of being choked by the thorny cares of this world (Matt 13:22) and missing out on the good news of the kingdom.

But can't churches with property consider accepting a reasonable sum of money from ministries leasing out their space? In some cases, yes. But prayerful considerations need to take place. A church considering leasing out space should consider one basic criteria: Will the charging of rent for the use of my facility lead to an expansion of the kingdom of God, especially regarding the furtherance of the Great Commission? If so, then charging rent may be justified. The challenge is understanding how to discern and honestly answer this question.

If a church is (and has been) diminishing in size and relevance for an extended period, and the rental income is focused solely on economic survival of a dying congregation, then charging rent is inappropriate. This is especially true if the congregation is using the power associated with their ownership of this property as a means of retaining the most optimum and convenient use of the facility, and thus requiring the new congregation to use the facility during the least optimum and inconvenient times. This is often the case when older white congregations seek to maintain control to accommodate their twenty-to-thirty-person congregations during prime Sunday and weeknight hours, while the tenant—often a growing ethnic church of a hundred to a hundred fifty—is relegated to 2:00pm Sunday services and intermittent and infrequent use of the facilities.

For the good of the gospel, churches in demographic decline need to be very careful not to maintain a stranglehold on resources they can no longer fully use. It may be time to have a hard conversation about who must increase and who must decrease (John 3:30).

Here are some guiding principles about an ideal leasing situation:

1. Money is not a concern for the church that owns the property.
2. The space benefits an organization that has significant mission alignment with the church that owns the property.
3. There are no unspoken expectations associated with the lease arrangement.
4. The leasing organization uses the space responsibly.
5. Use restrictions on the lessee are not onerous.
6. A healthy power dynamic exists between the church and the lessee.

We are human and deal with human institutions. Getting as close as possible to these goals will result in the highest probability of success for a lease agreement. Overall, the best option is the ethical option which ensures the property is being used. A church building or land that is not used is wasted.

The risks of a leasing option are the inverse of the ideal situation:

1. A church that is desperate for funds is more likely to seek an agreement that financially squeezes a lessee. They may expect that leasing revenue will solve other fiscal problems. Both realities are to be avoided. The former is just wrong; the latter is likely misguided.
2. A church that leases to an organization that has a significantly divergent mission may end up in a contractual relationship that develops significant strains.

3. A church with significant "unspoken expectations" for its lessee or for the effects of a lease agreement is likely to be disappointed. Such a church is likely to frustrate their lessee by putting inappropriate pressure on them beyond the explicit conditions of the lease, eliminating any intended sense of goodwill.
4. A lease to an organization that does not use the space responsibly is likely to be viewed as a failure for the church that owns the property. Developing mutually respectful relationships between leaders and creating explicit guidelines as part of an agreement can be helpful in preventing such a problem.
5. No church that leases its property should seek to take advantage of its position of power, but should seek to benefit its lease partners and, when appropriate, elevate their needs above its own.
6. Of course, leases involve all the normal risks associated with a contractual agreement, and problems can be avoided by consulting the appropriate legal and real estate professionals.

Despite these risks, the biggest danger lies in doing nothing and leaving the property resources of the church unused by the church and inaccessible to surrounding community. The best time to start a conversation about when to lease or lend out part of your church property is the instant you have a church property. There is no way any church is fully able to utilize all its resources. Partner with others as soon as you can. As 2 Corinthians describes it, there is a pressing immediacy to our work in God's present work. "Now is the accepted time" (6:2 NKJV).

Leasing church property is important for proper stewardship and effective mission for any church, but, of course, it requires many careful considerations and carries some significant dangers. There are amazing opportunities through leasing church property to extend the work of the gospel and bless others. I've worked with several churches to sort through the details of the process and set them up for success.

❧

If you don't have property, then you already know how challenging it can be to run an organization without your own space. A lot of time and energy goes into finding a space, and then a lot of ongoing time and energy go into prepping and cleaning up that space at every use. Finding a good fit up front with a property owner to lease from limits the challenges of this process. Leasing space from other churches may be the perfect solution for your needs, but it also can be a nightmare.

Knowing what to look for in a partner church is necessary for a successful leasing arrangement.

The right space involves more than a good location. It's probably best to think of the right space being a product of three things: location, value, relationship. And the element that is most often neglected is relationship, because it's harder than location and value to quantify and objectively discuss. But those relationships are the secret sauce to a successful lease.

Building a relationship with another organization before you enter a contract with them is crucial for the success of a space-sharing agreement. This will allow you to understand whether your missions align, whether they have significant unspoken expectations of the relationship, or if they are pressuring you to do things that go beyond your contract. Having a relationship ahead of time will allow you to notice possible red flags and hopefully avoid an abusive or manipulative relationship. It may also allow you to construct a contract that is less onerous for your church. If the location and value are right but the relationship seems iffy, don't sign on the dotted line. Waiting to sign a lease until you create a more significant relationship will ensure that the ultimate agreement works for everyone.

Even if you need a space in the short-term, you might prefer the stability that comes with longer-term attachment to a space, and perhaps some of the benefits that come from owning your own space ultimately. Sometimes these priorities can be addressed in the single solution of a "rent-to-own" agreement. This type of arrangement can be particularly helpful if you are not quite yet ready to own, but plan to be within a few years. Your ministry is ramping up. If you can find a church that is moving towards the point of needing to sell, you might be able to construct an arrangement that benefits you both. Lease-to-own agreements can be complicated and require a great deal of due diligence, but for the right partners, they can be a perfect fit.

6

Parables on Leasing

When we are committed to do God's will and not our own, we soon discover that much of what we do doesn't need to be done by us.

—Henri Nouwen

"It's all about who you know."

While this phrase often contributes to homogenous echo chambers (in which the best and most qualified people don't get a voice because they aren't well-connected), this idea also carries some positive connotations. Business works best when the professionals within them know each other and develop partnerships to tackle big tasks—it takes a "team lift" to move a boulder. And as business experts have long taught us, leaders must first cast a vision before businesses can work together well and turn a profit.

The church, though, is different. Unlike most businesses, the church is propelled by faith-based values and not financial gain. Additionally, the church is not a place but a people. It is the gathered saints of God, where the God of the gospel is freely witnessed to and in which all participate by their love for each other and their neighbors. As such, the church is also held to high moral and ethical standards by its king.

That same living Lord who communes with believers by his word and the Spirit has placed us in the world. And this wider world—whether it acknowledges Christ or not—has been given varying senses of God's multifaceted, common grace. In the Christian understanding of the best aspects of the secular world, it is through this unknown, but democratized grace that unbelievers move towards and love their neighbors.

Since we don't live in God's world apart from those in it, it makes sense for the church to identify and partner with groups in their surrounding communities that are effective in making life better for all people. If these groups share and demonstrate a love of justice and equity, churches can better accomplish aspects of their respective missions by working together. In showing our love for the world, we demonstrate who God is and why faith in Jesus matters.

Partnerships between the church and non-profit organizations must be thought of more as friendships than business arrangements. This is not to say that these relationships ought to be taken on apart from good business principles and basic legal restrictions. But partnerships between the church and other non-profit organizations are best conceptualized as friendships because of their local character, focused concerns, and close working relationships. Like any human bond, they require careful, intentional fostering. There's frequently a give-and-take that extends beyond the formally agreed-upon contractual terms.

Questions to Ask When Selecting a Lessee

- Does partnering with this group enable us to further expand the love of Christ?
- Does the group have a good reputation in the community?
- Does the lessee have a proven track record of success across the demographics of our community?

- Is our leadership unified that partnering with this group is a good idea? If not, why? Do dissenting voices pose a long-term risk to a successful partnership with the leasing group?
- Have all legal and financial precautions been adequately considered by our leadership team?
- Are our church's expectations about how the lease will positively and negatively impact the church reasonable?
- Does the leasing group have an established point person that can be contacted before, during, or after any time that they use our church's space?
- Does the leasing group understand, support, and respect the mission of our church?
- Does the leasing group see any special value in hosting their ministry or non-profit activity in our specific church?

The Story of Oakland Bayview Fellowship

Around the turn of the twentieth century, a group of believers banded together to form Oakland First Church of the Nazarene. This diverse group of believers gathered and grew through two world wars, experiencing rich ministry opportunities. During the tumultuous 1960s, Oakland First Church moved from its location near Lake Merritt to a more affluent area in the Oakland foothills, changing its name to Oakland Bayview Fellowship.

At first, the move revitalized the church. The previous years had seen declining numbers, as more and more congregants moved out of the Oakland urban area. But in their new locale, they not only benefited from new members but from some dynamic pastoral leadership. Like many revitalized churches, over time, the movement began to lose its momentum. Numbers across the board dwindled. By the turn of the twenty-first century, Bayview was in crisis.

Around 2010, a new interim pastor was sent into Bayview to begin the work of revitalization, but there wasn't much of a congregation left. Space was freely available throughout the week, so Bayview decided to lease out much of its facilities.

A growing preschool was selected as the new lessee. The group was providing a valuable service to families in the surrounding community, and Bayview was in support of its basic mission. Caring for the vulnerable was a shared value for both the church and the school. Like so many churches, Bayview also quietly hoped that they might be able to bring young families into their dying congregation. This became Bayview's primary plan: to expand its base to survive.

A lease was agreed upon, previously unused space began to be used throughout the week, and people buzzed around the busy preschool Monday through Friday. Additionally, the funds from the lease agreement provided the church with a massive financial boost. But Bayview's larger plan for church growth didn't pan out. Despite efforts and high expectations from Bayview's leadership, the parents who brought their children to preschool were not interested in attending church. The anticipated surge of new members did not materialize.

Unfortunately, the funds gained from the preschool ended up becoming a crutch for the church to continue as it was—a final measure of life support to sustain what is. Bayview had taken a step towards the community, but the expectations of how the church would benefit were unrealistic. Larger, structural issues remained. Despite the influx of funds, Bayview's congregation continued to decline. New missional opportunities were not engaged. Bayview died.

As is almost always the case when churches attempt to revitalize, Bayview's story is something of a mixed bag. Bayview may very well have had positive motives for welcoming in a preschool to its space, but in the life of Bayview as a church, it turned out that the money gained from the lease wasn't primarily what the church needed. The church needed to die in much bigger ways to comprehensively reform its ways of *being* the church. And when that didn't happen, Bayview eventually had to close.

While the story of Bayview is sad in many ways, it may be considered profitably now. First and foremost, the reasons for leasing a church must be established clearly ahead of time and rooted in a proper sense of mission. When a church decides to lease to an organization, the motivation must be first and foremost to serve the other. The priority of leasing must not be to gain from the lessee but to bless them. The church's business is to share the life of Christ, not to find ways to prop itself up for the sake of survival.

With the right motivation and mission, it is possible to lease out space to a preschool and, correspondingly, to see church growth. Nazarene District Superintendent Albert Hung saw it happen in his own church, which he pastored for years. It takes "coordinated effort and prayer and intentionality" to minister to families who are visiting a church due to their preschool connection, he said in an interview. The problem with too many churches is that their members "are not personally involved in outreach and building relationships with outsiders. They expect people will come without putting in the relational investment."

Just as the preschool at Bayview didn't lead to a surge in membership, neither will other lease situations—unless church members actively engage their neighbors. For a church to realize a connection between leasing space and membership growth, the church must first commit to doing the work of the church, apart from anticipated gains because of their service. This is the upside-down nature of God's kingdom.

Oakland Bayview Fellowship: Appraisals and Contingencies

- Cultivate a service mindset when entering a lease agreement.
- Monetary gain does not indicate growth.

- Set realistic expectations about community partnerships.
- If survival is the goal, you are missing the point.

The Story of Centerville Presbyterian Church of Fremont

Fortunately, another church offers a more useful example of creative use of space. Such a vision only comes to fruition as the result of intentional, experienced pastoral leadership. Centerville Presbyterian Church sits in the heart of Fremont, California. It has a storied past, with years of faithful presence in the surrounding community.

Pastor Greg Roth came to Centerville in the 1980s after serving overseas on the mission field. Pastor Roth completed his seminary training at Fuller Theological Seminary and began ministering with the homeless population of downtown Glendale, California. In that context, he learned the importance of teaming up with organizations outside the church. This included not only a network of relationships with local community leaders but also the city manager's office. When he arrived at Centerville, Pastor Roth already understood the importance of the church's presence among the least of these (Matt 25:40). As it turned out, Centerville was already growing in this understanding, too.

As Pastor Roth took on his new leadership role, he found that many members of Centerville already were working to meet their community's needs. Some of these needs didn't take much imagination to discern. For example, early on in Pastor Roth's ministry, the surrounding area of Fremont was known as "little Kabul," as there were more Afghan immigrants in the Fremont area than elsewhere in the Western hemisphere. Befriending and serving the Afghan community was a natural call. Centerville created a path-to-citizenship program for those seeking permanent residence in the United States. The response was positive, and many found new citizenship in the States.

Centerville's congregation had also long considered various ways to use their space generously. Most notably, before Pastor Roth arrived, the congregation was involved in a program called Centerville Free Dining. Each year thousands of free meals were routinely provided directly out of Centerville's facilities to those in need. The ministry was a sustained, long-term success. As members of the congregation interacted with more and more unsheltered and vulnerable members of the community, they got in the habit of befriending those who didn't formally belong to the church. As exciting as this was, Pastor Roth imagined even more ways for his congregation to share the love of Christ to Fremont. There were still scores of unmet needs.

In the process of meeting the needs of people on Centerville's streets, Pastor Roth made connections with leaders of other nonprofits and churches in town. He joined the largest Rotary Club in the area and quickly struck up a friendship with the police chief, the school superintendent, and others with untold influence in the community. As it worked out, Pastor Roth gained these new friends' trust and became something of an informal chaplain to the group. He started getting invitations to serve on different community boards and was asked to join a task force to study homelessness.

While these new community connections were often at the forefront of his mind, Pastor Roth was careful to prioritize his work as Centerville's pastor. As Pastor Roth officially took on his position at Centerville, he found some cracks in the foundation of the congregation's internal relationships. Despite good work in the surrounding community, several key relationships had frayed and needed pastoral attention. Pastor Roth knew spiritually vibrant external mission starts with internal harmony. Pastor Roth ministered to the people inside the walls of the church to ensure a healthy witness in the community.

Besides hosting listening sessions and making sure that people within the congregation were continuing to grow towards each other, he worked to learn and respect the church's history and traditions. Looking back, Pastor Roth realizes this was key to laying a groundwork for his largely outward-facing ministry. "If I wasn't honoring who they were, they wouldn't have gone anywhere with me," he mused. And he was right.

But to become truly effective in serving the *whole community*, Centerville needed more than a unified front. They had to partner with other groups to share the load. A plan to simultaneously expand on multiple fronts was put into place.

As Centerville moved forward into the 1990s, the leadership team and congregation agreed that building a community center would be an asset to the life of the church. With faith in God to provide, Centerville built a new 19,000-square foot family education building. The congregation was thrilled with the new space. Then Pastor Roth extended a challenge to the congregation. "Let's have outside groups use it, too," he suggested. That gentle prodding raised some objections. Wouldn't an influx of "outsiders" damage the new space?

As Pastor Roth watched conversations unfold, he saw that the whole congregation didn't necessarily want to do all that was needed to get there. The objections remained financial. Wouldn't sharing an expensive new facility inevitably cost additional money? Wouldn't items get broken and the floor scuffed up? Wouldn't the luster of the new building fade? Pastor Roth heard such concerns and hesitations by first listening. He then invited people to witness for themselves his proposed solution.

First, Centerville's leadership decided that when their space was shared, it needed to take place in ways that aligned with the church's overall mission. Second, and very importantly, they decided to lease out space to those who could pay and those who couldn't. The mission of the church was at the forefront of considerations, not what might be gained through leasing arrangement, and they planned to set aside money in the budget for inevitable repair costs and extra custodial care.

As it turned out, this helped people feel more generous. If something broke, money was already set aside to address the problem. When a water fountain broke, Pastor Roth wouldn't have to appeal to the congregation for repair funds. Years later, Pastor

Roth saw just how foundational this was for creating a spirit of open-handedness amongst his congregation. Having money set aside for maintenance and custodial services "helped everyone realize that you could have good management and be very generous with people in the community."

In each potential leasing situation, a church's leadership must decide if the connection established by leasing to a group sufficiently aligns with the church's overall mission. These considerations at Centerville would lead them to refer groups elsewhere. Equitable ministry still involves *intention and care*. The missional goals of the church are just and life-sustaining for all involved. In our present world, this still means acting as "wise as a serpent and harmless as doves," per Jesus himself (Matt 10:16 NKJV)

If a congregation or nonprofit group approached Centerville asking to host a long-term outreach in the shared community, there was a tried-and-true process for considering the request. First, Centerville's leadership would have preliminary staff meetings with them. In these conversations, the goal was to consider if they were compatible and if their needs and timing would work out with Centerville's own ministry schedule. Centerville could not lease out space that was already being used to serve the community.

Significantly, in these conversations, Centerville would also be very up-front about what kind of remuneration would be expected. In this context, they would also discuss how the other church handled issues related to childcare and accountability. Pastor Roth was experienced enough to know that those issues of accountability are often handled differently from congregation to congregation—and there must be safe, established protocols for accountability in overseeing children before a formal lease is even considered.

After Centerville's leadership wrapped up any meeting with the other ministry's leadership, they would bring their answers back to the larger elder board and prayerfully consider if they should move forward. If the leadership was convinced that a partnership might be established, the terms for a formal lease would be agreed upon and offered.

Centerville sought to create official, organic connections with whoever was leasing out the space. A member of the church staff attended all events hosted in the space. And if the lessees were going to try something new, a pastor would greet attendees and then hang around to observe and serve with the goal of discussing later what worked and didn't work. Centerville's policy was never "Here are the keys and have a great time."

Accountability always matters. And one of the best ways to keep everyone accountable, besides staying actively involved and present, is to make sure each lessee has a contact person that can be reached to discuss issues that inevitably arise when sharing space. Preferably, this person should be directly invested and involved in some facet of leadership. That way, if an appliance is left unplugged or a door is left unlocked, the contact person can be called on to resolve the issue.

Having this relationship for the long-term also pays off during an annual review and potential renewal of a lease. This yearly, formal sitdown allows a leasing ministry to evaluate how the year went with the lease and to find ways to better partner together.

Centerville's well-planned process was foundational for keeping nonprofit organizations operating smoothly out of their shared space. Long-term shared space may take work, but the return on the investment of time, energy, and resources is a kingdom profit.

Centerville Presbyterian Church: Appraisals and Contingencies

- Look for strategic partnerships unique to your community, faith-based and otherwise.
- Create a culture of hospitality that welcomes people from all walks of life.
- Adjust to meet needs unique to your community.

- Nurture internal relationships, so your congregation's health is reflected in service.
- Honor your church's history while looking to the future.
- Communicate expectations for sharing space clearly and thoroughly.
- Establish strong personal connections to ensure consistent, open communication.

The Story of First Presbyterian Church of Hayward

The world is connected as never before. Information once difficult to obtain is now readily available, and the daily choices for shopping or entertainment are seemingly endless. But amongst the abundance of images and information coming across our screens each day, many of us have gained a better sense of just how much different our neighbors' experiences are than our own.

We are all frequently guilty of forgetting to look out for the interests of others (Phil 2:4). With social media and more detailed data, we can see how the experiences of others differ from our own. The American Dream is more a distant myth than a reality for many. And for some, circumstances largely beyond their control have resulted in difficult economic and social conditions. With our vast access, we can now see this through our screens. But what are we to do as God's people? How is our mission directly impacted by our growing realization about the plight of so many of our neighbors?

The Gospel of Luke goes to great lengths to illustrate that the gospel of Jesus is truly good news for all people. The author takes special interest in highlighting the ways that God's Jubilee year has been actualized in Jesus' kingdom works.[1] The gospel is good news because the table of the kingdom is truly open to all people, no matter their social class, financial standing, sexual orientation,

1. Kraybill, *Upside-Down Kingdom.*

ethnicity, or gender. That we must be continually re-convinced of this reality reminds us how desperately we need the work of God's Spirit in our midst.

We are in an age of teams, not rugged individualism. Ministry partners can help churches run programs that assist underprivileged kids, feed the hungry, and help the unemployed prepare for and find work opportunities. Another way to extend the hospitality of God's people is to share space directly with the most vulnerable. While it might sound radical, it's a natural way to extend the welcome of God, even if it means relegating some of the control that churches have over their properties. Identifying and caring for at-risk populations may sound overwhelming to a church that is struggling, but it can be done well.

Pastor Jake Medcalf spent his early years in ministry working with the ministry of Young Life before starting a nonprofit organization for inner-city youth focused on youth development and urban farming. Later, Pastor Medcalf took a call at the First Presbyterian Church of Hayward, a historic mainline Protestant church. There was a missional heartbeat to the congregation, but as Pastor Medcalf arrived, he found the church was not very plugged in to the larger community.

First Presbyterian had once been a massive congregation in the 1970s, but like so many congregations across America at the end of the twentieth century, numbers had slowly dwindled. By the 2010s, First Presbyterian still possessed massive facility space on a large lot that their congregation was not using well. Unfortunately, many white families relocated as minority families moved into the neighborhood.

First Presbyterian realized that they needed to reach out, and they also needed a surge of funds each month to cover their long-term expenses. Before Pastor Medcalf's arrival in 2015, they had already begun leasing out a fourteen-thousand-square-foot administrative facility to Trader Joe's. Pastor Medcalf was glad to see the creative rental solution to unused space but came in with a new paradigm for long-term ministry. "We are going to measure our impact," he told the elders, "by what the non-Christian neighbors say about us."

First Presbyterian's previous neighborhood outreach attempts had involved inviting neighbors to a BBQ on the front lawn and providing a Thanksgiving meal to those in need. The larger missional focus remained international—helping kids in orphanages around the world. Pastor Medcalf had no problem embracing the congregation's passion to care for the orphan. However, he noticed that most people held local mission at arm's length. It was easy to meet neighbors once a year at a BBQ and to pack Thanksgiving dinners each holiday season, but what about the rest of the year? Pastor Medcalf began an intentional program that moved from "Bible-learning" to "Bible-doing," as he put it.

Pastor Medcalf expanded this paradigm by reorienting his people to understand their identity as the church. The heartbeat of the church, he said, is that "it is not about us." The reality that the church exists for its neighbors and not for its own sake was a rattling message for some congregants. Even as Pastor Medcalf taught and highlighted the opportunities to be the hands and feet of Christ, objections began to come from those on the fence. A chorus of critical voices loudly said, "What about us?"

First Presbyterian was at a crossroads. Pastor Medcalf had to stand his ground and meet the chorus of voices that were undermining the church's more comprehensive missional focus. It was a chance to illustrate the deep connection between discipleship and mission. Pastor Medcalf took steps to show all his congregation that moving outwardly was the divinely ordained way to renew the church. He grabbed onto a family metaphor. "The established church is like an older brother that objects when their parents bring in a second kid into the family. Parents don't love the older brother less, but yes, things may look different, day-by-day." This was a firm way of illustrating that some people didn't appreciate the renewed outward focus, and that was an opportunity for congregants to evaluate whether they were following God's calling.

Late one evening Pastor Medcalf sat in his office, working on a sermon to the sound of a thundering rain. After hearing a knock at the church door, Pastor Medcalf answered to find a soaking-wet unsheltered neighbor. The man politely explained that he was looking for a blanket because he needed to get through the cold, wet night ahead. Pastor Medcalf shared a blanket, received sincere thanks, and watched his new friend head back out into the downpour. *This should not be*, thought Pastor Medcalf.

In the coming days, Pastor Medcalf shared this story with the church elders and processed with them how theologically inappropriate it felt to not care better for this neighbor. The elders agreed. With scores of Scriptural commands to care for the widow, the orphan, and the undocumented, how could they do anything other than move out to shelter them?

Our Call to Defend the Vulnerable

Scripture is full of commands to protect the vulnerable and descriptions of God as the righteous Advocate of the underprivileged.

- "Open your mouth for the mute, for the rights of all who are destitute. Open your mouth, judge righteously, defend the rights of the poor and the needy." (Prov 31:8–9)
- "Learn to do good; seek justice, correct oppression; bring justice to the fatherless, plead the widow's cause." (Isa 1:17)
- "Father of the fatherless and protector of widows is God in his holy habitation." (Ps 68:5)
- "Given justice to the weak and the fatherless; maintain the right of the afflicted and the destitute." (Ps 82:3)
- "He [God] executes justice for the fatherless and widow, and loves the sojourner, giving him food and clothing." (Deut 10:18)
- "Blessed is the one who considers the poor! In the day of trouble, the Lord delivers him." (Ps 41:1)

- "I know that the Lord will maintain the cause of the afflicted and will execute justice for the needy." (Ps 140:12)
- "Religion that is pure and undefiled before God, the Father, is this: to visit orphans and widows in their affliction, and to keep oneself unstained from the world." (Jas 1:27)

With a plethora of underused space, First Presbyterian had a wealth of options for helping the unsheltered neighbors in their community. But frankly, it was a new experience for them. They decided to share space in the gym during the winter months. It came with a silver lining: creating a "warming shelter" was an opportunity for First Presbyterian to craft a partnership with the county. The county not only oversaw the process of setting up the warming shelter, but they also offered funds for its oversight. With scores of unsheltered neighbors visiting their facilities, First Presbyterian began to make new friendships. A couple dozen new faces appeared at Sunday services. The unsheltered community was feeling the welcome of God through God's people.

As First Presbyterian grew to embrace their new focus, energy to expand the mission grew. Pastor Medcalf realized that not only was there a need for shelter during the cold winter nights but during the day throughout the rest of the year too. For those unable to find employment, there were long stretches of the day when they needed a place to stay. As First Presbyterian discerned this need, the decision was made to open a drop-in resource center. Besides being a place that the unsheltered could charge their phones and escape the elements, it was also an opportunity to help those that were more transient.

The surrounding area's housing costs were prohibitively high, so the problem of equitable housing had long been on Pastor Medcalf's mind. He proposed a solution to the elders: why not use some of the excess space on the church lot to build tiny homes for permanent or semi-permanent housing? In faith, the church moved forward.

It took time to get the project underway. No one internal to the church knew how to seamlessly navigate the coding structure or the entitlement process, let alone the specifics of zoning, hiring a contractor, or all the other ins and outs of building the homes. Pastor Medcalf realized that he would have to become a quick student and rely on the expertise of others. To make the tiny homes a reality, Pastor Medcalf had to secure allotted space, sufficient funding, architectural plans, necessary city approvals, and a construction team.

Since the project took place on church grounds with church money, he also had to clearly communicate to congregants along the way. Not only did he need to make sure people were routinely aware of the plans, but he also needed to keep congregational support ongoing. His experience allowed him to understand that the church has a need for teams that understand the whole process, which led Pastor Medcalf to found Firm Foundation Community Housing to ensure a cohesive approach to the project from start to finish.

As First Presbyterian developed relationships with the county and other organizations, word spread, and other churches expressed interest in helping. When First Presbyterian crossed the finish line on the nearly two-year project, the full reality set in. The homes were awesome. They were comparable to studio apartments in the area and set in a nice location. The tenants were selected by another placement agency, and the federal government provided housing vouchers, paid directly to the church. Besides the valuable additional income accrued through the leases, a solution had been developed for long-term community needs. Pastor Medcalf had successfully executed his plan and developed a blueprint for other churches looking to replicate his model.

Pastor Medcalf's work illustrates another aspect of pastoral care. Sometimes the most loving thing a pastor can do for a congregation is to speak hard truth.

Addressing Conflict over Future Plans

Any movement forward in a church setting requires disciplined, courageous leadership. Keeping in view a few general principles can help see any conflict in context.

- Learn to take the temperature of the congregation. Negative feedback often grows with the size of a proposed change. It is normal to hear greater pushback when leading a congregation through a season of change—especially when it involves a recalibration of values, change of schedule, or new use of property. Take time to talk to representative members of your congregation about their perceptions. Learning how people receive messages can help future messaging, especially in terms of clarification.
- Work to turn down the temperature. There are always a heated handful of congregants that seem to pride themselves in being outspoken, even difficult. Winning over even a couple of those congregants can help to "turn down" the temperature of a congregation. Navigating conflict by publicly modeling humility and perseverance sets an expectation for anyone watching.
- Find your most comfortable level on the thermostat—and keep resetting the temperature. Initial opposing voices might be won over, but they may be replaced with others who hesitate about some facet of a plan's implementation. Identify the right temperature level and keep adjusting. Leaders can't take people where they haven't gone. Establishing healthy spiritual practices is foundational for long-term "temperature control" in a congregation especially when leading through change.

Pastor Medcalf had to show the church that they were called both to the furthest reaches of the earth and to their backyard. This full picture of missional outreach is exactly what we find in Jesus' command in Acts 1:8: "You shall receive power when the Holy

Spirit has come upon you; and you shall be witnesses to Me in Jerusalem, and in all Judea and Samaria, and to the end of the earth" (NKJV). Without the immediate outward focus, discipleship in relation to mission can become squashed down to the relative ease of cutting a check for someone else's work in a distant land. The church must always think and rethink mission. Feelings and fears can and must be overcome to embrace the fullness of God's missional calling on the church. The goal is faithfulness, not comfort.

First Presbyterian Church: Appraisals and Contingencies

- Cast a clear vision for community building.
- Speak hard truths lovingly while caring for the hearts of your listeners.
- Follow God's clear commands for caring for the vulnerable.
- Focus on people over profit or programs.
- Think outside the box of service to embrace sacrificial living.

7

Our Light Affliction

I cannot say whether things will get better if we change; what I can say is they must change if they are to get better.

—Georg C. Lichtenburg

I can say with near certainty that selling a church property is never anyone's first choice. We can plan to the best of our ability, but there is never any guarantee that what we expect to happen will occur. And because we can't predict the future, we sometimes need to react to circumstances in ways we didn't expect. This is not a failure. Sitting on unused property and refusing to sell out of fear is the failure.

Our calling is always to make the best, most faithful choices with the time, resources, and information we have available to us. And sometimes that means thinking about whether the most faithful course of action is to sell church property—not as a way of cutting our losses on a future that didn't pan out but as a way of doing the best with what we have for the good of others and the kingdom of God.

This is where the value of a recalibration of identity comes into play. What if selling was viewed as a chance to live out the larger mission that God has for all churches—growing, plateaued, and dying? When selling is considered through this lens, the whole process looks and feels different. It's possible to sell with success, because selling is a means to bless a broader community and even set up the next generation of believers for local missional success.

A church property sale can go awry if not undertaken for the right motives and purposes and with the right planning. So how should a church property be sold in in a way that most greatly benefits the mission of the church? How can a sale scenario failure be avoided? As with any creative use of church property, there are numerous pitfalls to avoid. The biggest mistake of all is waiting too long and missing the opportunity to do the most good for the mission of the church.

As I think back over my experiences helping churches sell properties, I can think of two different scenarios in which churches managed to sell in a strong way.

Proactive planning—rather than late reacting—sets up a church for selling success.

Although it's rare, I occasionally encounter pastors who intentionally position their congregations to prepare for the most likely five- or ten-year scenario involving the life of their church. Too often pastors and other leaders are so busy attending to the flock, they fail to take this long view and act ahead of time.

But those who take the time to see the drip, drip, drip of a leaking faucet realize that, unless acted upon, more damage is likely. It's important that leaders clearly map out what declining numbers mean for the future.

As has been previously discussed, learning to overcome denial is key. It means that churches can take pro-active measures far ahead of the pressure-cooker situation that many crisis churches find themselves in years later. For example, if a church was once a 1,500-member congregation but has more recently averaged 250 in attendance—and fewer and fewer are showing up to outreach events, small groups, and church potlucks—it's certainly time to begin an action plan.

Chances are you're thinking about selling church property because you realized that something about the life of your church that you or a previous generation envisioned is not going according to plan. Maybe attendance and giving are down, and you're looking for funds to shore up the budget. Maybe that parcel of land that was an aspirational or visionary purchase a few decades ago doesn't look like it will be needed, or maybe there aren't enough resources to do with it what was planned. If that's not you, and you're simply thinking proactively about the circumstances under which it would best benefit the mission of the church to sell church property before any problems arise, congratulations! You have the best chance of selling a church property with the greatest benefit to the mission of the church and the life of your community as a result.

Seeing signs of consistently unutilized space means it is time to act now.

For many pastors, the first clear signs of issues are declining attendance and decreased giving. But the corresponding reality is that the church property likely is already too large—or too much deferred maintenance exists—for the church to turn around. If there are empty, unused sections of a church building, unoccupied parsonages, or entire lots that are barely used, the writing is on the wall.

The good news is that if you are just noticing these realities, it's not too late to put together a plan that will succeed in benefiting the mission of the church and the life of your community. But now is the time to re-evaluate everything you are doing in light of your church's mission and goals to make sure you truly have God's desire to bless others at the center of your planning and strategy. As you think through whether to sell, your decision will be aligned with the mission of the church and the benefit to your community.

A church property sale should not be a Band-Aid for a church with a terminal diagnosis. Such a sale will not stem the ultimate failure of mission and execution, and serial attempts to prop up this body will continue to fail. This chapter is intended to help you think through how a sale can benefit and service focused mission. And the good news is, with the proper planning, tools, and resources you can learn whether to consider a church property sale, what that process might look like, and how to do it well.

At its most basic level a decision to sell is a decision of priorities. You are trading away property for something different that you value more. But how you understand the something different you get in the trade has everything to do with whether such a transaction will be considered a success. And there are many ways to understand what you might get from a sale.

What might you value more than your current property? Contributing to the success of the mission of the church to bless others? Supporting the flourishing of your community? Seeing the next generation fully resourced to seek and follow God? Or could it simply be that another property (or no property at all) would fit the needs of your church better than your current property?
If you think a property sale is in your future, consider your answers to these questions:

- Is your property still an asset?
- Is your current property a drain on your congregation rather than a boon?
- Have budget woes caused you to defer maintenance on your property?
- Or does maintenance cost a large percentage of your budget that would otherwise be spent on something more closely aligned to your church's mission?

- Do your most dedicated and devoted parishioners spend a lot of their time dealing with the building rather than ministering to people?
- Could selling your property free up their time so that they could be doing more valuable work for the kingdom of God?

The ideal selling situation is one that isn't rushed by fiscal emergencies or wracked by heated emotions, but it is generated out of a long-range, careful planning process which aligns with and supports the ultimate mission of the church. It also doesn't hurt for the property in question to be of significant value based on the local real-estate market and zoning. There are four factors that will increase your chance of a successful property sale: timing, clarity of intent, congregational support, and property value.

When all these factors align, your church property sale has the greatest chance of making a significant impact on your mission and beneficial effect for your community. No church is in a perfect situation. Typically, a good deal of work will be required to move into a healthier place on any one of these issues, and largely uncontrollable factors will determine your property's value. So, if we are clear-eyed about what can be done as far as it depends on us, under what conditions should we consider a sale of church property necessary?

Short answer: sell church property when it is in the best interests of the mission of the church to do so. If your church is strong, growing, and looking for opportunities to expand its mission and influence, that doesn't mean that selling a church property is not for you. Too often, sales of church property are seen as capitulation to otherwise unmanageable decline. However, certain kinds of sales can build on the successes you may already be seeing.

Also, if your church life appears stagnating, either for demographic or cultural reasons, and property is becoming a drain on the remaining witness and resources of your church community, a church property sale may be something to consider. Church property sales can turn a church's experience of dying badly into one of dying well while benefitting others or revitalizing a community. There are four ideal church candidates for selling.

Churches with more property assets and options.

The easiest selling decisions are the ones made at churches with multiple property assets. Any sale is a momentous and challenging decision, both financially and emotionally. It can make it much easier and less fraught if it doesn't seem like everything is riding on the disposition of a single property. A church with only its building is in a more difficult position than a church with a main building, an adjacent building for a school or functions, an empty lot, and a parsonage. Having a sub-dividable lot adds flexibility, and a partial sale is easier to pitch than a full one.

Any decision about the church building will elicit emotions related to the ultimate survival of the church community and will be wrapped up in memories related to that building. While churches with fewer assets may still need to sell, the situation is not ideal. Churches with many assets may not need to sell, although they are likely in a better position to do so.

Churches with in-demand property.

Sales are easier to set up when property values in your area are high, and property is in demand. Is your church property in downtown New York? Good! You're going to have a lot of people interested in buying your property. Is your church property in a rural area with declining population, declining industry and business, declining property values, and declining church attendance? If so, that is going to make a sale much more difficult.

Churches with unencumbered assets.

The easiest church property sales involve the least encumbered properties. Determine if there are any mortgages or liens that might complicate a sale. Many churches are not owned by the local congregation but by the denomination with which they are affiliated, which can involve approvals processes. However, on the plus side, many denominations have very robust governance supporting the disposal of church-owned real property. Looking into your denomination's resources and support processes as early as possible will save headaches later.

The kinds of sales possible may also be affected by the zoning of the property. Is the property zoned to allow new buildings, or alternate uses (residential or commercial)? Typically, the fewer zoning constraints, the easier it will be to sell the property, though this should not be viewed as a serious obstacle. Though zoning boards are often known for the difficulties they pose to developers, many will approve zoning changes if presented with a compelling case that the proposed change will benefit the community.

Of similar effect is the presence of issues at the property resulting from deferred maintenance. A property with no deferred maintenance issues is easier to sell, but deferred maintenance is not an insurmountable obstacle. In fact, many churches that are stuck with a building with significant deferred maintenance are the very ones most in need of a sale. The good news is that even though such properties can be hard to market, sales are possible, and there's no shame in walking away from a building for which you can no longer afford the upkeep.

Churches with property assets that are a net drain.

This last category has less to do with ease of sale and more to do with necessity. If this category is the one you identify with the most, all hope is not lost. If it seems like more and more of your time, energy, and money is spent dealing with a building that feels more like a burden than a blessing and pulls you away from the ministry you are called to, you should probably sell. Buildings that are a burden to the ministry of a church should be sold if possible, and ownership transferred to another party if a sale is not possible. Someone else, even another church community, may want the building and may be blessed by it. But whether anyone else wants it or not, it's just a building. The church is made up of people, not stuff. And if the building ceases to benefit people, then it needs to go.

Should you be one of these four churches, you may be considering selling. The process, however, can be cumbersome. Here are five general steps to selling church property that I developed while running DCG Strategies, my former firm.

1. *Understand your long-term vision.* It's vital that you and your congregation have a shared long-term vision before you engage in the real estate process. Starting with a focus on strategic discernment will help ensure your short-term objectives are met while maintaining the long-term goals of your ministry.
2. *Determine if you can sell it.* Find out who owns your church building. Autonomous, independent churches can make their own decisions. However, churches that belong to a denomination might not own the building and must work with the appropriate denominational bodies and follow internal legal governing rules to sell the building.
3. *Consider what you'll do with the money.* Denominational bodies usually won't allow you to sell a property and use the proceeds for operating expenses. In most cases, the funds must be used to purchase a new building, to support a community mission, or to contribute to other nonprofits. For churches that sell their buildings but still need a place to meet, it's important that you have a plan for your new space. Whether you find a place to meet that is free, rent or purchase a new building, or break up into smaller units and spread out in the community, identify your options before you put the building on the market.
4. *Hire an experienced church broker.* Traditional real-estate brokers and developers are strictly for profit and are trained to consider your situation with a transactional goal in mind, but an experienced church broker can help you understand *how* you want to sell the property. The right real-estate agent will analyze the market to land at the best possible outcome for the sale of your holdings, conduct a detailed analysis of the factors contributing to the sale, and enter

negotiations equipped with critical data points to understand the true market value while also considering that the goal of your sale might not be typical of other real estate deals.

5. *Protect yourself from risk and liability.* The paperwork involved in a real estate transaction can be overwhelming, and transactions involving church properties are complex. Sometimes the land a church was built on has deed restrictions attached to it, or the zoning might need to be changed if the buyer isn't a church. It helps to have someone act as your owner representative, reviewing all the documents, contracts, permits, and agreements to ensure a smooth outcome.

Many people feel a good deal of anxiety over large decisions, and particularly over decisions implicating large sums of money or legal issues. Church leaders and members are no different. Thankfully, most of the logistical and financial risks can be avoided by being informed, involving all necessary parties to the decision-making process early and often, and working with one or more competent and ethical real-estate professionals that specialize in church property sales.

Finding the right real-estate professional can be challenging. Some denominations have preferred providers that are pre-vetted, and I have many excellent colleagues who have aided churches through this process, but it can still be difficult to get the proper professional help to avoid legal and logistical problems. Many churches are understandably worried they'll be taken advantage of by an unscrupulous real-estate agent. Having a trusted professional provides a safeguard against selling for too little, being cheated in the process, or making costly legal mistakes.

Of all the risks in selling, however, the biggest risks lie in going through with a sale under terms that don't benefit the mission of the church and its community—or going through with a sale without adequate congregational stakeholder support. The one danger results in a failure of the mission, and by extension, a failure of the purpose of the sale. The other results in a fracture of the church community due to lack of understanding and buy-in. Both risks can be largely avoided by congregational support for a clear church mission well ahead of a sale so that the sale is both seen as a success by the congregation and is an actual success for the mission of the church.

8

Parables on Selling

Grief may be difficult to recognize in a church because its various expressions hit different people at different times.

—L. Gail Irwin

In the late 1990s, the Philadelphia 76ers appeared to be an NBA team on the way to greatness. Under the leadership of Coach Larry Brown, the 76ers' 1999–2000 season took them to the second round of the playoffs, where they expected to pass by the Indiana Pacers on the way to the Eastern Finals. But the Pacers' torrent of offense was too much for Philadelphia.

The next year was even more of a heartbreak for Philly fans. After an astonishing, record-breaking season, the 76ers pulled out narrow first- and second-round playoff wins over the Pacers and Raptors, respectively. Then, the 76ers met their greatest challenge of the year in the Eastern finals: the Milwaukee Bucks. After seven hotly contested games, the 76ers emerged victorious, marching on to their first NBA Finals in decades.

But the 76ers' offense was tapped out. The Los Angeles Lakers—led by future MVP Kobe Bryant—embarrassed the 76ers, closing out the NBA Finals in just five games. The 76ers returned home disappointed and spent.

In the years after this trip to the finals, the 76ers sputtered. Despite Allen Iverson's near magical offensive moves, the team couldn't find their rhythm. By the late 2010s, the 76ers had not made it to the playoffs in years. The loss of the 2001 NBA Finals became a distant memory in Philadelphia sports legend.

Through these years a mantra developed amongst Philly fans: Trust the process.

Given their losing record throughout most of the 2010s, Philadelphia gained better and better draft picks. Trades were made and recovery continued. By the early 2020s, the 76ers were back on the map as a playoff contender and a Finals hopeful.

As congregations, we must trust the process in selling, too. What seems like a loss now may end blossoming into a win in the future. And since the kingdom's own Cornerstone has a better perspective than any of us, trusting the process can be understood as part of the Spirit's work.

The Story of El Cerrito United Methodist Church

As the first decade of the 2000s came to an end, the historic El Cerrito United Methodist Church faced a crossroads. Once a vibrant and leading member of the community, a confluence of factors had dragged down the life of the church. Members were aging, some had died, and many had already relocated or left the church. New faces were not replacing old ones.

With dwindling numbers and mounting deferred maintenance, decisions had to be made. Should the congregation merge with another congregation? Should they move towards closing their doors entirely? Was there a way to revitalize?

It didn't take long for the aging group to realize that they couldn't let go of their shared life. Closing the doors would inevitably impact their ability to care for the oldest members. Why cut off a life that had so long been fostered through mutual sacrifice? The members still had hopes for a future growth. El Cerrito took intentional steps to befriend the community. They advertised a yard sale and offered up items to those who came. The congregation met as a group one Sunday morning and went to the local park. There, they had coffee and food and invited others to worship with them. No one came.

Margo Bennett, a long-time member, reflected on that rejection. "The reality that a lot of people had to face was that just because you open your doors doesn't mean that people are going to come. You've got to have something as a congregation that others want."

A merger was considered but rejected. El Cerrito wanted to live but not lose their identity along the way, so leaders began to walk through the discernment process. An interim pastor was assigned to help educate the congregation about the financial pressures, the challenges of revitalization, and the long-term challenge of caring for the building. It was tough to be confronted with these realities, but they were undeniable. After two years of consideration, the congregation voted to sell.

Selling Your Property Timeline

- Step One. 2–3 months. Work with pastor, congregation, and denomination to garner alignment and support for seeking options.
- Step Two. 3–4 months. Create and market a Request for Proposal to seek out options for consideration.
- Step Three. 2–3 *months.* Review offers for disposition of the property, select the preferred party, and finalize an agreement.
- Step Four. 2–3 months. Standard due diligence period including disclosures, title review, reports, inspections, assessments, and financing contingency.

- Step Five. 6–30 months. If a standard use permit is needed (e.g., for a private school), this could be 6–9 months. If redevelopment (e.g., residential development), anticipate 18–30 months.
- Step Six. 1–2 months. Work through final documents and financing to formally close escrow.

As a realtor came on board to help with the process, another local church heard about the potential sale and immediately expressed interest in purchasing the building. After some negotiation within the denomination, the sale was approved. The beautiful thing about this sale to another church was that it gave El Cerrito's members the peace and joy of knowing that their property would be used by another group of believers. The building would be repaired, and new generations of Christians would worship and serve within its walls. But there was still grief to process, especially with the impending loss of their building.

To help people deal with this loss and to mitigate trauma, Barbara Glendenning, the Chair of Trustees at El Cerrito, invited members of the congregation to help prepare for the closing. As people cleared out closets, classrooms, and other space, younger members were paired up with older folks. As they culled and cleaned, the older members of the congregation shared memories of the past ministries. Barbara encouraged people to take one item as a way of coping with loss. Professor Scott Cormode suggests that leadership relies on listening, and Barbara listened as congregants shared their burdens and felt heard.

The week after El Cerrito's building closed, the remaining congregation moved to their relocated space—the parsonage, which they still owned. With fewer than twenty active members, it made sense to share a small space for the time being. But as members trickled into the parsonage that first Sunday, Margo sensed fear. "People were very tender and afraid of what would happen," she reflected. The questions seemed to be, *Are we homeless? Will we still be attached and bonded without the building?*

To make matters worse, the neighbors around the parsonage were not only disinterested in the church; they opposed it. Hearing the elderly group sing hymns each Sunday morning was not appealing. El Cerrito would have to find a new home. Fortunately, another local Methodist congregation, Good Shepherd, reached out and offered to lease space to El Cerrito. Not only that, but they would even accommodate El Cerrito's weekly time of worship by changing their own worship time each Sunday. El Cerrito gratefully accepted the offer.

In what became a beautiful and surprising development, the two congregations found much in common. As their relationship evolved, El Cerrito and Good Shepherd became one under the new name "Open Door United Methodist Church." El Cerrito's journey had come to a peaceful completion, birthing a new space for a growing church and creating a new congregation. As new faces joined the table at Open Door, they used utensils that had once fed members of the former congregations of El Cerrito and Good Shepherd. Their legacy and their stories continued to live on.

El Cerrito's journey forward is encouraging, even beautiful, in hindsight. But, like nearly every other story, along the way, any number of factors could have taken them off course. The initial key to the successful move forward came from leadership that was intentional about moving the congregation to a point of decision.

As the congregation grew to understand the depth of the financial and organizational crisis, a positive movement happened. People took ownership of their role in the process and showed up at meetings, expecting to have a voice. Thinking back to some of these congregational meetings considering the future of the church, Barbara remembers people with no active involvement in the church appearing and strongly asserting things like, "Yes, this church must keep going on." Some of the feedback was critical without being helpful. El Cerrito's leadership and faithful congregants had to learn to cut through the noise and stay focused.

Understanding that the church is the gathered people of God and not a building was a game-changer for the members of El

Cerrito. Going through the denominational discernment process helped members realize their deep love for one another. This special, precious love for God and one another was a shared bond that extended beyond just simple memories of life in a building. As this took hold, Barbara shepherded the flock by walking beside aging saints. If they hadn't had this space to grieve and honestly express frustrations and fears, they may have never finally relinquished their grip on the building.

In hindsight, Margo can now see that this part of the journey wasn't just a process to get through but was an integral part of growth. We can't live into a new future until we've learned to reckon with the past—including the space on which it has played out. It takes time, trusted partnerships with lay leaders, and a long-term intentional process to move a congregation through any transition. Pastoral care is always a balancing act, but the special kind of juggling act to make these kinds of moves possible should be readily acknowledged from the outset.

Amongst the internal challenges of deciding how to move forward, El Cerrito's leadership also had to manage external oversight. Barbara quickly learned the importance of being well-organized and thorough in her communications and presentations to committees and superintendents. Church leadership at the upper levels often moves slowly, despite the best of intentions. Churches can and should learn to advocate for themselves. In the case of El Cerrito, Barbara had to be direct and to re-explain situations to administrators to make clear timetables, needs, and intended outcomes.

The path that El Cerrito took to merge with another church only came after a faithful response to the divine call to sell unused space to a growing congregation. In that vulnerable place, the aging and fragile group experienced God's rekindling work.

The renewal that El Cerrito experienced only took place because of their initial sale. That itself required a humble recognition that their historically white church did not match the surrounding community and that the Chinese Evangelical Church did. The CEC had leased for years and were so blessed to be able to purchase this building as a permanent home. The fact that this sale was to a church outside the UMC was also a testament to how the death of one congregation can give life to another.

> **El Cerrito United Methodist Church: Appraisals and Contingencies**
>
> - Take ample time to decide whether a sale is the right course of action.
> - Allow space for individual and communal grieving regarding the loss of physical space tied to memories.
> - Stay open to possibilities that may not be obvious solutions at first glance.
> - Understand that the church is a people, not a building.
> - Invite everyone to be a part of the change, and clearly communicate with leadership, administrators, denominational overseers, and congregants.

The Story of Journey of Faith

A friend of mine moved to the Philadelphia suburbs and visited his local library two blocks from his new home. After a self-guided tour, he approached the circulation desk to request a library card. "I'm sorry, that's not possible," the librarian told him. "You aren't from here."

As it turned out, my friend's new home was one street over the township's line. He was an outsider, ineligible to partake in township resources, even though he could walk to the library in five minutes. To make matters even worse, the township pool—which was across the other side of his neighborhood—was also in another district. He couldn't take his kids there without paying an astronomical fee. The lines had been drawn and there was nothing he could do about it.

Sadly, these types of boundaries aren't just found in arbitrary township lines outside Philadelphia. Congregations often communicate explicitly or implicitly that outsiders aren't welcome in their church space. Perhaps most commonly, they communicate that certain cultural standards must be met to enter and receive welcome. The welcome of God too often comes with an asterisk and a plethora of tiny print.

Lindsay Hill, a leader who builds tiny homes for the unhoused population, shared with me that even church signage sometimes reflects this mentality. "There are all these regulations around space," she says. We have all these church signs that say, "no dumping," or "no loitering," or "don't park here." Like the library in the Philly suburbs, we create restrictions that become obstacles to relationship. Mission to the other becomes subsumed somewhere far under the umbrella of church cultural comforts.

The priority of outward-facing mission is too often dismissed, only to be replaced by inward-focused programs. We even come up with names to excuse this focus. How often do family ministries programs bridge the life of a family unit with a truly long-term outward-facing mission? Sadly, it's far too rare. I see nothing wrong with ministers working to help families develop together into disciples, but programs too easily become entertainment venues, not breeding ground for mission.

Beyond the problematic relational dynamics in many churches, there's a deeper structural problem that impacts the future life of many, many churches. Established, albeit declining, congregations don't want to welcome in younger, often minority-led, congregations.

If the wave of the future of global Christianity continues to be found in countries within the southern hemisphere,[1] we'll likely see minority congregations in North America working to evangelize us. White populations are now the mission field. But as this happens, we'll continue to see young, growing minority congregations in need of space to meet. A unique opportunity exists to share space with those who aren't yet able to afford it. Rather than

1. Sanneh, *Whose Religion*.

closing our doors, will we look to bless the entirety of the church, globally speaking, whenever possible?

Journey of Faith Nazarene Church has a rich, long history beginning with its joining of two churches in Fremont, California, following the post-World War II economic boom. By the time Pastor Joe Shreffler came to Journey of Faith many years later, they were property rich but ministry poor. So, Pastor Joe turned the congregation towards their neighborhood.

While the congregation prayerfully considered how to proceed over the course of several years, Pastor Joe worked to create signage that faced the community rather than just the passing road. "That new name and new signage was," Pastor Shreffler reflected, "a change of our personality as a church. We wanted to open ourselves up to the neighborhood." Pastor Shreffler was challenged by a member of the congregation who was upset because her late father had created the original sign. Pastor Shreffler had to find a way to bridge the past with the future and did so by creating new signage for all the congregations who were using their space while keeping the older sign intact.

While Journey of Faith opened their space to the community and two young minority congregations, bigger problems began to arise. Despite owning prime real estate property, Journey of Faith had deferred basic maintenance issues for years. The parsonage was rented out to generate further income, but they couldn't create much revenue. A cellphone tower contract was signed. Meanwhile, Journey of Faith considered selling parts of the property. But this met stiff resistance from both denominational overseers, who hesitated to sell any real estate, and city officials. Journey of Faith was stuck with an aging building, three financially strapped congregations, a long-term cell tower agreement and major long-term renovation needs.

One day, the church fax machine beeped and buzzed with an unsolicited offer to buy Journey of Faith's property. Pastor Joe tossed the offer in the recycling pile. After more than a dozen such offers came in over the fax machine, Pastor Joe realized that Journey of Faith should consider selling outright. The real estate developers realized they were in a prime location, and Journey of Faith had a limited financial future, given the massive costs they faced to keep the building open.

Pastor Joe had to be honest with himself, with God, and with the board of the church. He shared, "I'm stretched out as far as I can go. The building is going to start falling down around us. And we are sitting on property worth a lot of money. We must start praying and thinking about how to move forward."

For three years, Pastor Joe worked, prayed, and developed relationships with people in the community who could help overcome obstacles to make a sale possible. But Pastor Joe wanted to not only sell with an eye towards future growth but also future congregational death.

God redeemed the maintenance deferrals of the past. Even as Pastor Joe and Journey of Faith continued to bless their community by lending out space for a dog park, baseball practices, and community gardening, they kept up their long-term promise to partner with ministries in local Spanish-speaking churches. The costs to do these ministries didn't make sense on paper, but they did to a kingdom-focused church. The sale of the church would have to bring in sufficient funds to make up for the lost time and money.

A Christian realtor offered an arrangement where he would bring in experts to maximize the value of the property by obtaining approvals for a residential subdivision and to obtain a release from the long-term and onerous cell tower agreement. But to make this plan work, a new site needed to be identified and purchased, and a clear plan developed to secure denominational approval.

Pastor Joe wasn't trying to kill Journey of Faith as a church. But even as he thought about the future and how he would bring on board the denominational leaders, whose support he needed to secure the sale and purchase of a new building, he wanted to make sure that the minority congregations he so loved also had a future home.

Initially, there was some pushback. But then, a small miracle happened.

"We found a building in Hayward that would allow us to eventually replace ourselves with a bilingual community. That was original vision I had and God was bringing it to pass."

As Pastor Joe and his professional realtor located a facility closer to the heart of the Latinx community they so longed to serve, opposition softened. Those whom Pastor Joe expected to voice the loudest opposition began to get excited about the new site. The sister congregations were glad to be partners, even to share a load in the long-term upkeep of the property. Through a joint effort, founded in love and a sense of mission, the future was wide open. Journey of Faith would live in their new location for as long as God wished. And then a new generation would replace them.

When Journey of Faith moved to its new location, that sign came along. It's possible to creatively integrate old pieces of the past into new things that God is doing. Nostalgia often serves to pin down the people of God and prevent them from looking to the future, but memories matter. But Pastor Joe managed to navigate these realities, specifically by inviting people along to see that God's bigger plan built on past faithfulness.

Reflecting on the process, Pastor Joe captured the beautiful, mysterious work of God:

> What we've learned through all this is that God's ways are higher than our ways because He sees a future that we cannot see, one that is hidden from us because it's "over the horizon" from where we are. But, if we trust Him, we always get to see His hand move in real time. That alone is worth all the uncertainties we face.

Journey of Faith: Appraisals and Contingencies

- Create a space that is forward-facing and welcoming to the community.
- Be very cautious about entering into long-term cell tower agreements.

- Be realistic about capacity regarding maintenance costs.
- Don't allow maintenance issues to hinder mission.
- Growing in one way sometimes requires death somewhere else.
- Trust that God has a timely and blessed plan that can bridge the past and the future.

The Story of the Sisters of the Holy Family

Marcus Tullius Cicero is known today as one of the great thinkers and orators of Western civilization. Not only was Cicero a master of rhetoric, a lawyer, and a respected statesman, but also a brilliant philosopher. He was a genius. He lived at a particularly interesting time in the history of the Roman Republic—a time marked by political intrigue, civil war, and the infamous assassination of Julius Caesar. But Cicero's fame extends to us now in part because, well, he wanted to be known. While Cicero's ends were self-serving, he understood something important: we all contribute to our own legacy.

For the Christian, this future legacy ought to be intentionally shaped as a witness to God's kingdom. Our names and reputations will fade with time. And that's okay. Like John the Baptist, our own plans must be shaped by fidelity to Jesus: "He must increase, but I must decrease" (John 3:30).

Perhaps the best way to begin thinking about crafting a legacy is to start with the present. Revisiting the attitudes that we've adopted over time can lead to more fruitful outcomes for the future of the church. In my experience, many of us often live life assuming our local church is just *there*. In our minds, local church spaces are apportioned to some mental place where we lump other permanent, immovable fixtures, those things we imagine will remain forever untouched by changing times.

Churches hold a place in our living memories because of the ways the events that have taken place within their spaces have shaped us. We know that people move on, pass away, and that no church congregation will ever be numerically identical from one year to the next. But in our minds church structures should be preserved at all costs because eternally valuable things have occurred within their walls. They become a shrine to the past, as we once experienced it. These attitudes are deeply problematic.

Our attachments and memories need to be re-remembered in light of God's greater work, greater calling, and cosmic story of redemption. What is God calling us to pursue with our space now and for the long term? As we think about the ways these realities impact our ability to intentionally craft a legacy that meets the future needs of our communities, District Superintendent Albert Hung's reflections are again valuable to consider. We receive these spaces as a gift and only for a time. At no point are any of the talents gifted to us by God ours, full stop. The Lord will demand account of how we've used his gifts.

A profitable way to think about the nature of gifts and our role as stewards for the future comes from a phrase in Paul's letter to the Corinthians: "for I received from the Lord what I also pass on to you."[2] Just as the message of salvation is received from those faithful saints who came before us, so we must loosen our grips, and look to pass on a faithful legacy to younger and future believers. We truly can work, by the power of God, to craft a legacy in thoughtful, joyful ways, even if we are approaching the end of our personal or corporate lives. The stories of faithful saints who have done just this can help us imagine our own possibilities anew.

The Sisters of the Holy Family is an order of the Catholic Church that was originally founded in the late nineteenth century. Throughout the twentieth century, the Sisters expanded beyond their original base in San Francisco and reached across California to surrounding states and even to Alaska and Hawaii. Over their years of ministry, the Sisters' work has benefited thousands of children and underprivileged members of the community.

2. The language of "receive" and "hand on" plays on the Pauline notion of tradition regarding the Lord's Supper, as seen in 1 Cor 11:23.

In recent years, the median age of the Sisters of the Holy Family has increased as their resources have dwindled. They are gaining fewer new members and the needs of their older members are naturally changing and growing. But rather than shrink away from mission and wallow, the Sisters continue to think and act out of a sense of calling.

The Sisters have always viewed their ability to reach the world with God's goodness and love as not being inherently linked to the life of their Order. In keeping with their vows of giving all of themselves—including their property—to God's service, they have learned how to carefully structure plans for this long-term vision. Even if they themselves may no longer be present to participate or even experience the blessings inherent in such selfless giving, they remain determined to leave a legacy for others to experience God's grace, love, and mercy.

The Sisters' current strategy is the result of patient planning and learning from their past. To plan for a new line of strategic initiatives, they drew on past experiences. Beginning in the 1980s, the Sisters began to carefully consider how to use their real estate to bless others. They first sold a portion of their land to a Montessori school. Then, the decision was made to sell another portion of the land to help create affordable housing.

The subdivision and sale of the land to the Montessori school was relatively uneventful. The school benefitted from the bountiful land and existing education building. Both were leveraged to become an important and successful part of the community. The school remains to this day and was recently augmented to include a middle school building.

The affordable housing, however, was more challenging because neighbors were fearful of those who might soon live in their midst. The City Council had to address concerns. But the Sisters' careful planning proved to play a huge role in showing those who were concerned that the homes would be relatively low-density and provide two-story townhomes for seniors and families in need. Despite political pressure, the Sisters were able to push the project through the City Council's turmoil.

The lessons learned from these past sales showed the Sisters the need to carefully proceed with any future ideas—this time with a better idea of how to engage with the City Council.

In their preparation for the future, the Sisters recently undertook a full review of their portfolio with the help of professionals. The overarching goal of this plan was to provide qualified nonprofits with valuable real property assets that could be resourced to carry these ministries well into the future. In doing so, the Sisters committed to structuring these transitions so that the lease and/or purchase payments would not create a financial impediment to the nonprofit's ability to sustain their ministries into the future.

Since 1951, the Sisters had called their property in the Mission San Jose area of Fremont home. Situated on almost fifteen acres of the picturesque and historic Palmdale Gardens, their property included their seventy-five-thousand-square-foot "Motherhouse" and two historic Tudor-style homes. In recent years, the Sisters realized that their beloved Motherhouse was no longer suitable. Flights of stairs and communal bathrooms were not conducive to the aging population.

The Sisters began to gain the realization that if they didn't make concrete plans for the future of the Order, someone else would. They realized "we needed to move forward," Sister Gladys Guenther, President of the Order, reflected. So, in accord with their commitment to caring for the underprivileged and the earth itself, the Sisters began the long road of merging their future strategic planning with the funding potential of their real-estate holdings. Their core planning principles included a special focus on providing shelter for the unhoused and for preserving and providing public access to the six-acre Palmdale Gardens.

After more than seven years of planning and obtaining the requisite land use approvals from the City of Fremont, the final plans revolved around the subdivision of the property. The Sisters retained 2.6 acres to allow those remaining on the property to age in place. Three cottages were constructed, each containing fifteen bedrooms. For the first time in decades, each Sister could enjoy having her own bedroom, bathroom, and in-room kitchenette.

Each cottage also contains a communal kitchen, dining room, and living room. As the need for the cottages dwindles, they can be sold, used by another religious order, or repurposed as community living for other seniors. A chapel was also constructed on the property.

To fund these improvements, 1.1 acres were dedicated to the restoration of the two historic Tudor-Style homes, which were then sold to private homeowners. A 5.66-acre area that included the Motherhouse (which had become functionally obsolete) was sold to a private homebuilder who ultimately developed and sold eighty-seven homes. The money from the sale of this portion of the property was used to fund the construction of the cottages. But the Sisters were intentional about whom they worked with and the way they used the proceeds. The sale not only secured a renewed space for the Sisters, but it also provided $3.4 million for the construction of affordable rental units for homeless veterans. Additionally, the Sisters wanted to do something in line with their long-term mission to preserve the environment.

The 5.5-acre Palmdale Gardens, including grottos, the three-hundred-year-old trees, two ponds, and a grove of cypress, was a perfect vision of how the Sisters wanted to maintain green space for the future. With financial help from the homebuilder who purchased parts of their property, the Sisters gifted Palmdale Gardens to Garden Conservancy, a 501c3 nonprofit whose mission is "to preserve, share, and celebrate America's gardens and diverse gardening traditions for the education and inspiration of the public." Palmdale Gardens would remain a place of natural beauty—a picture of the Sisters' own commitment to life, not only of nature, but of their shared life in Jesus.

The Sisters knew how to capitalize on lessons learned from the past in their quest for future life. Because of tumultuous times dealing with the Fremont City Council in the 1980s, members of the Order knew what to expect, how to build bridges, and the necessity of planning early and often. Reflecting on the final stretch of planning, Sister Gladys realized that it was important to not be intimidated by the process of dealing with the city. But legacy planning took place in and through this process precisely because of a clear commitment to mission.

The Sisters relied on people that were known in the community as trustworthy, competent professionals. Aside from the City of Fremont, there was a Historical Architectural Review Board, and a need to learn all kinds of details about zoning, building codes, and construction management. Sister Gladys engaged with attorneys, brokers, and realtors. "We established a team," she said. "Everyone on the team had a sense of contributing something bigger than themselves."

The Sisters implemented a long-term solution by working with competent professionals, who committed to careful planning and thoughtful implementation. For the Sisters, strategic sale of portions of their property was a win. It allowed the community to bless the neighborhood for the long-term, even as the Sisters remain in their midst.

Sisters of the Holy Family: Appraisals and Contingencies

- Consider legacy in the broader sense of God's kingdom purposes, not as an individual desire for future remembrance.
- Work with trusted professionals to make sound financial decisions around property.
- Build bridges with community leaders to ensure legacy includes a good reputation among your neighbors.
- Even when selling, decisions must remain driven by mission.

9

Pressing on Toward the Goal

You can, you should, and if you're brave enough to start, you will.

—Stephen King

Choosing to pursue a path that directs a church at large to embrace their end is personally painful and difficult. Job security is often on the line. In the case of a decision to close a church's doors and sell the property, memories of work and investment in a congregation may soon be lost to the past. But even this pain must be contextualized in view of God's calling and mission. Pastor Josh Wroten helpfully comments, "The church does not exist to provide employment for a pastor. The pastoral role exists to equip the church for the ministry."

For some pastors, thinking about this end may lead to a moment of self-realization. A pastor's job is to shepherd the flock by obediently making disciples, not to maintain security and coast into retirement. This outward-facing focus seeks to imitate Jesus, who came to seek and save. In other words, the internal and external aspects of the church's mission are unified around a common divine purpose.

Pastors who are serious about repurposing property for kingdom purposes should understand the path ahead is multifaceted and requires careful planning. So where do we start?

Step #1: Brainstorming.

Thinking about the possibilities of renewed mission to the community should be exciting. But how this intersects with your own situation and your own church properties is the million-dollar question only you can truly answer.

I hope you're inspired by the ways that churches are already choosing to act. In every case I've described, pastors, lay leaders, and denominational leaders were able to use property in creative ways. Your situation may well overlap significantly with one (or more) of the stories in this book, but don't make the mistake of trying to replicate someone else's story.

On a related note, this is one of the reasons that resources about church revitalization are often unhelpful. They encourage dying churches with stories of successful "turnarounds," implicitly suggesting they should serve as models for revitalization. Pastor Joe Shreffler tells a cautionary tale that illustrates this point. During his pastoral ministry, Pastor Joe met with a group of church leaders. Many of the books they chose to study were written by pastors who had managed to lead their people out of decline and into greater spiritual vibrancy. But, as Pastor Joe noticed, the context in which those pastors and authors did their respective ministries often differed significantly from his group's context. "Look," Pastor Joe told the group, "I have nothing against a guy like Andy Stanley. If I was going to plant a church or help to revitalize a suburban church in Atlanta, Georgia, I would look to his work with great interest. But this is a model that only works in a certain context." One size does *not* fit all.

If you see a great principle in this book, but it doesn't sufficiently align with where you, your congregation, and your properties are, move on. Productive brainstorming must be open to discovering dead ends. You'll quickly discover that you may think you know where you're going, but you probably don't. Not yet anyway. It takes some time to consider all your options.

Brainstorming Tips

- Create a culture that is open to ideas. Brainstorming is most productive when used as a routine practice, not a one-time activity.
- Carve out time in your schedule not only to think through church problems, but also potential long-term solutions.
- Construct a system for keeping a record of your brainstorming sessions. Envisioning solutions on paper or a white board will ensure all parties are on the same page, have time to reflect, and don't miss important points.
- Cultivate the right environment. Some people think well in nature. Others like a dark room with quiet music playing. Some prefer their office. Wherever you choose to do your brainstorming work, make sure you do so in an allotted space, for a set time, without the possibility of interruptions.

Step #2: Conducting an Assessment.

Experts can help you assess your church's property health and create a roadmap for moving forward with your facilities to both death and new life. Bringing in an external professional to consider the specifics of your church's situation is critical. Don't make the mistake of thinking that a handyman from the congregation—as gifted as they may be—will be able to comprehensively assess property issues, let alone a set of solutions for repairs. An outside expert is a must.

As you look to bring on leaders with a larger paradigm shift in mission and use of real estate, Pastor Shreffler suggests strategically bringing up an undeniable area of need to elicit support for a larger review. For example, in a board meeting, you might say, "Looking over the choir loft, I see what appears to be black mold. I'm concerned about this issue. We need to bring in an expert to assess the sanctuary's deferred maintenance issues." A board that sees an undeniable problem will likely act on it.

For many congregational situations, it makes sense to not only hire an external professional to assess deferred maintenance, but also to bring in a larger church assessment team at this stage. While a church assessment costs money, the results will provide a greater sense of the condition of a church's property and the state of the people who worship within them. A trained outsider brings a new set of eyes to the situation.

According to DeMott et al., a facilities assessment report will include an "introduction, brief history of construction and maintenance, summary of findings, description of existing conditions, causes of problems, recommendations and remarks, cost estimates, photographs, drawings" and even some additional reports from other specialists.[1]

An assessment should also include a clear picture of the demographics and needs in the surrounding community. Data sets from an assessment can be overwhelming. Ask about the implications of the numbers when receiving these reports. This kind of interpretation offered by an expert is just as important as collecting the data itself.

Having firm data in hand about the state of your church is sobering. But knowing the true state of things helps a board or group of lay leaders understand that change must be pursued. The roadblock of denial that we talked about before is often naturally overcome when a church's leadership team recognizes the problems facing a congregation and asks their lead pastor to act on this assessment. When a board or leadership team gains this level of investment, they begin to own the process that stands ahead. With

1. DeMott et al., *Holy Places*, 198.

leadership support to seek out solutions to pressing problems, a pastor can move forward, empowered with knowledge and the backing to make real change.

Step #3: Gaining Community Support.

Your larger community, not just your leadership team, must be brought on board. Pastor Shreffler suggests making a congregational announcement about the expert findings. It is important to clearly signal that the leadership team is moving together to work out meaningful solutions. In this context, questions will naturally come.

Allowing people to be heard is a way of affirming they matter in God's kingdom, but doing this is often difficult. Even when a solution has not yet been officially posed, people don't like to hear that their beloved church is declining. Congregants take this news personally. After all, they have invested their own resources into making a sanctuary their home, often for many years. Upon hearing news of trouble and the need to act, people will lash out, vent, express denial, outrage, or perhaps most commonly, dismiss the findings.

By the power of the Spirit, congregational leadership will meet people where they are, gently listening and showing them sufficient details to make clear the status of the church. With grace and time, even some of the most obstinate naysayers can see the truth. Consistent, compassionate messaging will help people accept the reality of decline and the need to act.

Moving forward with congregational support also involves inviting people into the process. Pastor Joe suggests wedding this process with prayer and Bible study. At the beginning of each such pastorally led class, he implemented a rule: anytime a problem was mentioned, a corresponding solution must be proposed.

A Bible study like this might also be strategically focused on discipleship and mission. Why not begin an intentional process of helping people connect the dots between a renewed sense of identity and their future outward action as a group of Christ's followers? There are many good book studies that might be undertaken. But, as we've already learned, any gains in knowledge of Scripture's calling must be geared towards praxis. Convincing people to grab onto a paradigm can be helpful, but showing people how beautiful a renewed walk with Jesus into the community is? That is the way to make sustaining change.

Step #4: Bringing in The Experts.

Bringing in a faith-based consultant that can address emotional and spiritual challenges may be helpful. It depends on your context as to how soon to bring in a real estate agent, a broker, an attorney, a tax expert, or a contractor. You'll want to start talking with the right people to gain clarity on the path forward. Many times, a real estate broker is best suited to help envision the process of a bright future.

Time and again, I've heard pastors reflect, "The best thing I ever did was hire that broker. They were worth every penny." Bringing in the right professional isn't an extraneous part of the process; these are the people that pave the way to a successful future. A neurosurgeon isn't an extravagant expense or a luxury when you have a brain tumor—and neither are these experts and specialists. They play an invaluable role in equipping your congregation with the information and action steps needed.

When interviewing prospective realtors, the church must first make sure they are dealing with someone who specializes in commercial real estate. Ask questions. Assess if the realtor understands the critical questions facing the life of the congregation. And do they seem to care? It takes some digging to discern how well-equipped the realtor may or may not be to handle your situation. Does the realtor have the necessary tools to help the church optimize their use of real property assets in furtherance of the gospel?

Some real-estate agents may pressure you to act quickly and to sign them on right away. This is a bad sign. Take a few days to consider their presentation and any materials they provide. It's always good to interview more than one agent. This will give you time to follow up and ask for references. If the broker is as good as they sound online, people in the community will independently attest to their excellence. Here are some questions to ask:

1. What is your real estate expertise?
2. How many years do you have in the business?
3. How many congregations have you served?
4. Where were these congregations located?
5. What success stories most illustrate your vision for our congregation?
6. What unique concerns do you have about our property?
7. What strengths do you see in our property?
8. How long do you think the sale will take?
9. Do you have connections with prospective buyers?
10. How do you think the faith community plays a role in the public good?

The real-estate agent plays a critical and sensitive role. It is one that should be afforded only to those who are deemed not only competent from a real-estate perspective but conscientious in terms of placing the mission of the church ahead of their own financial gain. If you sense an agent's focus is wholly on dollars, then that broker is not the right person for you.

Church leaders need a trusted partner to help them navigate all the possible ways they may use their real property in new ways. They must support the pastor's work. They should understand the need for overwhelming congregational support. They should explore options for the future use of the church facilities. It's crucial that they work to leverage property for outward-facing ministry revitalization and not look to gain the biggest cash offer on the market.

The goal is the redirection of a church's ministry, or the giving of life to others in the process of approaching death. The broker must be able to effectively explain the ins and outs of all merging, leasing, or selling options.

While these decisions are always difficult, profound blessings await churches on this resurrection journey. Richard Rohr defines this challenge eloquently:

> I am afraid many of us have failed to honor God's always unfolding future and the process of getting there, which usually includes some form of dying to the old. In practical effect, we end up resisting and opposing the very thing we want. The great irony is that we have often done this in the name of praying to God, as though God would protect us from the very process that refines us! God *protects us into* and *through* death, just as the Father did with Jesus. When this is not made clear, Christianity ends up protecting and idealizing the status quo—or, even more, the supposedly wonderful past—at least insofar as it preserves our privilege. Comfortable people tend to see the church as a quaint antique shop where they can worship old things as substitutes for eternal things.[2]

Once a broker is engaged, church leadership can consider a preliminary report detailing the most likely options for the property. This will paint a clearer picture of the hard numbers. With mission in mind and a sense of the estimated value that a merge, lease, or sale might garner, leadership can move forward at peace. God's good and present future is at hand.

2. Rohr, *Universal Christ*, 93–94 (emphasis in original).

10

Testing Everything, Holding Fast What Is Good

There are two kinds of fools: one says, "This is old; therefore, it is good"; the other says, "This is new; therefore, it is better."

—William Ralph Inge

Many times, churches are not truly independent when it comes to property or even the ministers who oversee them. The structures of church polity differ from denomination to denomination, and nothing that follows can fully account for these meaningful differences. One denomination may hold legal rights to the property. Another may have rules in place that make name changes difficult. And still others have long-term denominational goals that serve to pressure churches to focus on a particular direction. So, for a church within such a denomination, the question must be: how can I partner with my denominational overseers in my creative and missional use of church property?

In recent years, many organizations have worked to make denominational structure a force for good, which opposes individual corruption. But the power dynamics that are still seen in the business world often shape us, whether we realize it or not. This is especially evident when denominational overseers are tasked with evaluating churches that wish to proceed in a new and creative way.

There are often a handful of leaders within denominational structures that have unspoken power. Sometimes it is simply because denominational committees get into rhythms and routines; the experts in the room are deferred to out of habit. Individual church leaders that seek out help are not meeting with enemies, but oftentimes, opposition is invisible. The reasons that a denominational oversight committee or person chooses whether to embrace an idea may be unclear due to the unspoken rules and unexpressed norms.

Therefore, much like relationships between local church leaders and the non-profit organizations that they choose to serve, communication and friendship must be fostered. We need one another as brothers and sisters who share in commitment to God's big story. Learning to address these power dynamics is important. Knowing they still exist, despite our best efforts to overcome them, helps us understand how to work effectively.

Within most committees, there is at least one person who plays the role of gatekeeper. Pastor Shreffler describes the situation well:

> That "initial gatekeeper" may be . . . a bishop or district superintendent or even a chairperson or influential member of the board—the one who brings the proposal to the board or committee. That person almost always sets the tone for how the proposal will be perceived. Such boards or committees are appointed or elected by the larger organization and, as a result, they feel an obligation to support the perspective of the body that put them into authority.

Identifying that person is the first task. Take time to carefully notice who makes up the board that will need to approve your work. Do you know the members? Who would you guess is most influential? It may sound like extra work, but it's imperative that you attend a meeting not related to your own ministry's future missional real estate plans. Your job is not to ingratiate yourself but to look with new eyes on the people who carry the weight to approve or disapprove local church plans. Whether by observing as an outsider or by seeing it in your own meeting, you'll identify the way a gatekeeper contributes to the conversation and often the decision.

Look at how differently a meeting went for Pastor Joe when he came in with the support of a gatekeeper:

> I came into my interview. The circle was large, and I was on the spot. But the elder pastor in the room gave the affirmative nod. He introduced me with a clear signal to all in attendance. "Joe is one of our bright spots. He's been doing good work. Does anyone have questions?" The questions were brief, and my interview was a success.

While it's tempting to become cynical, a clash that often occurs between local leaders who are ready to pursue mission and their denominational overseers is not necessarily due to a desire to maintain the status quo. It's often a difference in perspective.

These leaders are used to seeing things from the top. They sit above the entire forest. This positioning has its strengths; sometimes overseers are familiar with emerging networks of pastors that have interests in similar ideas. They might even connect two churches that are a strong fit for a merger, or they can anticipate changing economic conditions that would impact the viability of a church plant. Unfortunately, sometimes this big-picture vision makes denominational leaders inwardly focused. They see the dangers facing many congregations, and they work to make sure congregations are actively avoiding what they perceive to be a very threatening risk.

Local leaders often see things differently precisely because they are on the ground, amidst the trees. They know the people, the needs, and the micro context of the ministry. For the responsible, faithful shepherd, mission has been taken seriously.

One common roadblock occurs when your missional reengagement resembles work that someone else in your district, presbytery, or larger national denomination has (unsuccessfully) attempted. In my experience, denominational leadership has an uncanny recollection of any such cases that went wrong. Your ideas are likely to be associated with another church's, a church that you may have very little in common with. Your best way forward is to convince the committee that you're able to take the *specific* path that you, your staff and leadership, and congregation have committed to follow. But this is exactly where, in a paradoxical sense, denominational oversight is a deeply good thing.

As frustrating as it might feel at the time, this kind of leadership requires more preparation, conviction, and planning, of which your church will greatly benefit. Denominational interactions foster accountability. If you don't have the necessary information or the right process, it's the responsibility of your denominational overseers to help you reroute. The body of Christ is designed for interdependency, and we all benefit when seemingly disparate parts work together. At its core, denominational leadership can and should make you better and sharper. The fruits of this labor are a better long-term process, clarity, and success.

When you have properly researched and gained assessments from seasoned professionals, you know more about the project than those who oversee you. It's easy to stand up under scrutiny and have the enthusiasm for a bright future. And when you're approaching a committee this way, they'll naturally take note.

When you receive formal approval, see if this accountability can develop through regular check-ins, preferably in-person. The denominational overseers may be busy, but they should take initiative to routinely follow up. In an ideal context, this long-term relationship should be with the goal to help you, the local pastor, with any bumps in the road that you encounter. When pastors and denominational leaders work well together, everyone wins.

Conclusion

In the end, Jesus wants to be embraced . . . those who would accent doctrine and dogma and have very little love in their hearts and very little courage to fight for the poor—Jesus would be the first to say . . . that's sounding brass and a tinkling cymbal. That's empty. It's vacuous.

—Emma Green

I recently listened to a sermon in which the pastor addressed the congregation by saying, "You can help to flip the script and change the narrative." I turned up the volume, hopeful at this introduction.

To my shock, my brother in Christ boldly claimed that the church can and should help itself by intentionally focusing on those within the four walls of a local church. He went one step further. "Tune out the world," he said. "Love one another instead. It just hurts my heart to hear the negative press about the church."

I was stunned. There was no admission that perhaps the American church has negative press for a reason. There was no acknowledgement of the systemic abuses that were, even at the time of this sermon's delivery, coming to light in a variety of churches, including in that pastor's own denomination. And the message to the attentive congregation was to come in and take part in the church's programs, rather than engaging outside the walls of the church. The implication was clear: don't complain if you sense something amiss. "Change the narrative," the pastor said, "by finding something good to say."

Sadly, this message has become a common response to some of the biggest problems facing the church—the refusal to change course, the refusal to take the path of the Emmaus Road with Jesus.

As I've pleaded throughout this book, we *must* name and repent of our shortcomings by reapplying ourselves to Christ's outward-facing mission. But none of us can truly correct course, accept the death of previous ways of doing ministry, and live into God's resurrection power without God acting. To willfully die to self means to entrust ourselves to the God of the resurrection. And God decides when and how to grant what is promised. There's no shortcut to the process. To bear (resurrection) fruit, death is required.

To take one of the paths I've described in this book assumes a Spirit-led process of repentance and wise, faithful discipleship. I hope that amid the stories you've read, this point wasn't missed. Revitalization of a local ministry doesn't occur without the Spirit's mysterious, often veiled, work.

One of the temptations that pastors face each day is to try to do ministry in their own strength. We face an Enemy who quietly urges us to ignore the call of the gospel. And besides the spiritual battle, it's naturally hard to die to self.

I don't mean to be negative. But shoring up our shrinking base, looking inward, and demanding that people not critique us for refusing to take part in the common good are hallmarks of spiritually unhealthy churches. And the watching world knows it. Even now, large swaths of American pastors vocally oppose basic preventative health measures in the middle of a global pandemic. Our churches have become some of the loudest echo chambers for conspiracy theories, anti-vaccination advocates, and political extremism. God cannot be pleased.

Here's my diagnosis of our situation, as best as I can give it: We have much to repent of, corporately and individually. Negative press about the church isn't killing the church. It's our willful refusal to repent and change course to meet the moment God has given us. And so, unwillingly, the (spiritually declining) local church comes to an organizational end. What has been true internally becomes revealed externally in the form of vacant (or nearly vacant) space.

In the meantime, despite the commonplace that I've sought to address in this book, there are already individual Christians and congregations that are moving in the right direction. I'd be remiss if I didn't bring them into view. Many are drawing on divine strength and actively resisting the nationalist, xenophobic discourse of so many unhealthy American churches. They gently come alongside weaker brothers and sisters and help them see the way of Christ is different than the one they knew before.

These modern-day saints share something else in common: they are outwardly focused and deeply missional. They decided to love people without anticipated gain. Are we joining them or merely observing from the sidelines? This is a question that every Christian, every leader, must answer.

Frankly, this is a much different way to think about the Church's calling than we are used to hearing. Too often, we fall into the trap of thinking that successful ministry looks like large numbers of attendees, salvations, baptisms, and giving. But, as I hope you've seen throughout this book, faithfulness to mission revolves primarily around the free offer of Christ's gospel through expressions of unconditional love to our neighbors. Loving God by loving our neighbors is integrally a part of what it means to be truly human. Wedding this to God's larger mission must be the focus of every church leader before we begin to imagine such a scene in our own context.

I hope that this book has sparked your imagination, and I hope you have a new picture of what faithfulness to God's calling can look like, especially with church spaces.

Maybe it goes without saying, but in my understanding, fulfilling the mission of God doesn't look like "winning." It's not an intellectual triumph in a fierce theological or personal debate on social media. In all points, it embodies the humility that Jesus exhibits. And when we inevitably fail, we can repent and get back on track. When we are faithful, reliant on God, and sacrificially serving, it may feel hard. But along the way, the Spirit gives us a foretaste—personally and communally—of the wholeness of future resurrection life that is to come. Perhaps this is why Paul could describe the Spirit as the "down payment of our inheritance." The same Spirit who is so closely associated in Scripture with God's own future is also the One who carries us, by faith, to that place.

Practically speaking, what does the Emmaus Road look like, day by day? In my experience, it looks like an early morning gathering to pray with other believers, hold one another accountable, and decide on which needy neighbors to serve. It looks like long afternoons of cooking meals and sharing them with neighbors that can't get out of their homes due to illness or age. It looks like sharing our spaces expecting nothing in return.

I know it's hard, but divinely wrought faithfulness to the ancient call of Christ means giving up what is ours and freely sharing it in Jesus' name with the least of these. Sharing real estate space is a key way to accomplish this. God's Jubilee, God's missional self-giving, and God's gifts to the church can and must work together for God's plans to come to pass.

I'm not calling for the church to look like the progressive, secular world. We are remade in the image of Christ, not the most winsome personality or cause of our day. But sometimes, it appears that God's gift of common grace to those who do not claim the name of Christ is more fruitfully accepted and used than the grace received by those who call themselves followers of Jesus. That reality should humble us.

God's work in the world involves the instrumentality of many human agents. The mission of God isn't limited to those in the four walls of the church, but it must include them. Denial of Christ's call to die is what I'm begging my brothers and sisters to prayerfully overcome. Resurrection life doesn't come about to those who don't willingly walk the Emmaus road.

The mission that we are called to go on together demands an urgency. This requires we build coalitions, networks, and partnerships that are just, ethical, and fundamentally committed to blessing others.

This is not new. Amid exile thousands of years ago, God commanded Judeans: "Seek the peace of the city where I have caused you to be carried away captive, and pray to the Lord for it; for in its peace you will have peace" (Jer 29:7 NKJV).

The mission we're on now means faithfully showing our fellow-citizens that we are present for their good, even when they might not yet see it. The church will be seen in a favorable light over time when we humbly refuse to embrace the hesitations of people who are persuaded by toxic theology, self-serving politicians, and pseudoscience. We aren't called to surrender God's future by bowing to those whose political bent preys on others by pretending to suffer a lack of self-perceived freedom. God does not invite us to participate in the divine life to oppress others, even while claiming we are the ones being hurt.

As I've argued throughout this book, that means the church (as it too often exists) must die. And, as I hope is sufficiently clear, this death isn't the end. Death, discipleship, and mission belong together, with resurrection awaiting all who hope in Christ. Sometimes that means the metaphorical resurrection of a church's local ministry.

In my understanding of Jesus' teaching, discipleship means seeking out the way of Christ—a willful self-denial of rights, personal interests, and power. In offering us a share in the resurrection, God brings us to God's future—a time in which every part of the created order will be justly, peacefully reordered. Our efforts and work must align with that reordering. Otherwise, how can we truly pray, "Thy kingdom come, Thy will be done, on earth as it is in heaven"?

By loving and leading well, we can fulfill God's calling and show the next generation how God leads and acts in the everyday.

In this, we'll follow the apostle Paul, who handed down to other believers what he received from the Lord. We'll echo his own words to the next generation of believers: "Be imitators of me, just as I also am of Christ" (1 Cor 11:1 NASB).

The death of the way Americans have done church for decades is here. Let us not mourn, for it doesn't mean the end of the kingdom of God. But let us strive towards expansion of Jesus' own interests and family.

There will be no magic solution to future growth and kingdom expansion. There will only be the culmination of faithful, obedient choices that almost invisibly combine to create a new world. This is what agency in God's kingdom looks like: beautiful, personal, loving acts by individual believers in community, with and for others.

The aging church now has a unique opportunity. For those retirees with time, sufficient energy, and deep, focused concern about the future that will unfold after their time, a "second mountain" peaks over the horizon. In secular terms, David Brooks discusses the joy of having the time to take on a larger purpose in the final stage of life.[1] To me, this description is beautiful because it not only meshes with my own stage of life, but it aligns with what I have been describing in the aging church. There is an opportunity that we in the "golden years" must not pass up.

What if, as District Superintendent Albert Hung reflects, a new generation of younger believers is gifted with the wise, intentional counsel and actions of an older generation that has freshly re-found their way? My own imagination prickles with images of intimate gatherings of older and younger Christians, carefully listening to each other and thinking about how to join forces in pushing the faithful on to the promised land. I delight in the thought that many second mountains may cumulatively be climbed by a sea of grey-haired faithful saints, eager to invest in the future life of God's kingdom, both within and without the walls of the church.

1. Brooks, *Second Mountain*.

To make that happen, obedience to the Spirit's calling is all that's needed. The task is in front of us all—young and old alike. And the world—God's own world—is groaning for its renewal.

New Testament scholar N. T. Wright captures another, complementary understanding of the Christian's calling: "Our task as image-bearing, God-loving, Christ-shaped, Spirit-filled Christians, following Christ and shaping our world, is to announce redemption to a world that has discovered its fallenness, to announce healing to a world that has discovered its brokenness, to proclaim love and trust to a world that knows only exploitation, fear and suspicion."[2]

May that vision grow to fruition, in our local congregations, even now. In the Name of the Father, Son, and Spirit. Amen.

2. Wright, *Challenge of Jesus*, 184.

About the Author

Dominic Dutra has dedicated his life to helping others. He has proudly served his community as a two-term member of the Fremont City Council, his church in various volunteer roles, and his alma mater (Santa Clara University) as an adjunct faculty member. As an educator, Dominic works to equip and cultivate excellent, virtuous business leaders, preparing them for the challenge of business in the twenty-first century. As the former President and CEO of Dutra Realty, Dominic seeks to leverage his business and real estate expertise to make our world better. Dominic founded 3D Strategies with this in mind—people matter more than profits.

Dominic's lifelong Christian values and his passion to serve organizations have inspired him to create real change at local level. In this vein, Dominic is committed to optimizing the underutilized and surplus property of faith-based non-profits and public organizations. Dominic thrives in helping such organizations become more fiscally sustainable, even as they become more effective in meeting their long-term goals and accomplishing their respective missions.

Dominic has a BS and an MBA from Santa Clara University. He and his wife, Lisa, have been married for thirty-five years and have raised two children—Tricia and Gabriel.

Bibliography

Allison, Dale C., Jr. *The End of the Ages Has Come: An Early Interpretation of the Passion and Resurrection of Jesus*. 2nd ed. Eugene, OR: Wipf & Stock, 2013.

Bandy, Thomas G., and Page M. Brooks. *Church Mergers: A Guidebook for Missional Change*. Lanham, MD: Rowman & Littlefield, 2016.

Barth, Karl. *Deliverance to the Captives*. Eugene, OR: Wipf & Stock, 2010.

Benner, David G. *The Gift of Being Yourself: The Sacred Call to Self-Discovery*. Downers Grove, IL: InterVarsity, 2015.

———. *Surrender to Love: Discovering the Heart of Christian Spirituality*. Downers Grove, IL: InterVarsity, 2003.

Bonhoeffer, Dietrich. *Life Together*. Translated by John Doberstein. New York: Harper & Row, 1954.

Brooks, David. *The Second Mountain: The Quest for a Moral Life*. New York: Random House, 2019.

Cartwight, John, and Chris Hulshof. *Everyday Bible Study: Growing in the Christian Faith*. Nashville, TN: B&H Academic, 2019.

Cormode, Scott. *The Innovative Church: How Leaders and Their Congregations Can Adapt in an Ever-Changing World*. Grand Rapids, MI: Baker Academic, 2020.

DeMott, Nancy, et al. *Holy Places: Matching Sacred Space with Mission and Message*. Lanham, MD: Rowman & Littlefield, 2007.

DeYmaz, Mark. *The Coming Revolution in Church Economics: Why Tithes and Offerings Are No Longer Enough, and What You Can Do about It*. Grand Rapids, MI: Baker, 2019. Ebook.

Edmondson, Amy C. *Teaming: How Organizations Learn, Innovate, and Compete in the Knowledge Economy*. San Francisco: Wiley, 2012.

Elsdon, Mark. *We Aren't Broke: Uncovering Hidden Resources for Mission and Ministry*. Grand Rapids, MI: Eerdmans, 2021.

Gorman, Michael. *Becoming the Gospel: Paul, Participation, and Mission*. Grand Rapids, MI: Eerdmans, 2015.

Hays, Richard B. *The Moral Vision of the New Testament: Community, Cross, New Creation: A Contemporary Introduction to New Testament Ethics*. New York: HarperCollins, 1996.

Hoang, Bethany Hanke, and Kristen Deede Johnson. *The Justice Calling: Where Passion Meets Perseverance.* Grand Rapids, MI: Brazos, 2016.

Irwin, L. Gail. *Toward the Better Country: Church Closure and Resurrection.* Eugene, OR: Resource, 2014.

Jones, Jeffrey D. *Facing Decline, Finding Hope: New Possibilities for Faithful Churches.* Lanham, MD: Rowman & Littlefield, 2015.

Jones, Jeffrey M. "U.S. Church Membership Falls Below Majority for the First Time." *Gallup*, March 29, 2021. https://news.gallup.com/poll/341963/church-membership-falls-below-majority-first-time.aspx.

Kraybill, Donald. *The Upside-Down Kingdom.* Harrisonburg, VA: Herald, 1978.

Kübler-Ross, Elizabeth. *On Death and Dying: What the Dying Have to Teach Doctors, Nurses, Clergy, and Their Own Families.* 40th anniversary ed. New York: Routledge, 2009.

Lipka, Michael. "Mainline Protestants Make Up Shrinking Number of U.S. Adults." https://www.pewresearch.org/fact-tank/2015/05/18/mainline-protestants-make-up-shrinking-number-of-u-s-adults/.

Longman, Tremper, III. *The Bible and the Ballot: Using Scripture to Make Political Decisions.* Grand Rapids, MI: Eerdmans, 2020.

Lowe, Stephen D., and Mary E. Lowe. *Ecologies of Faith in a Digital Age: Spiritual Growth through Online Education.* Downers Grove, IL: IVP Academic, 2018.

Malphurs, Aubrey. "The State of the American Church: Plateaued or Declining." http://malphursgroup.com/state-of-the-american-church-plateaued-declining/.

Newport, Frank. "Five Key Findings on Religion in the U.S." https://news.gallup.com/poll/200186/five-key-findings-religion.aspx. Accessed 22 July 2021.

Nouwen, Henri J. M. *Can You Drink the Cup?* Notre Dame, IN: Ave Maria, 2012.

Peterson, Eugene. *Practice Resurrection: A Conversation on Growing Up in Christ.* Grand Rapids, MI: Eerdmans, 2013.

Piketty, Thomas. *Capital in the Twenty-First Century.* Translated by Arthur Goldhammer. Cambridge, MA: Harvard University Press, 2017.

Rainer, Thom S. *Autopsy of a Deceased Church: How to Keep Yours Alive.* Nashville, TN: B&H, 2014. Ebook.

"Religious Switching and Intermarriage." https://www.pewforum.org/2015/05/12/chapter-2-religious-switching-and-intermarriage/.

Rendle, Gil. "The Legacy Conversation: Helping a Congregation Die with Dignity." *Ministry Matters* (blog), February 1, 2011. https://www.ministrymatters.com/all/entry/716/the-legacy-conversation-helping-a-congregation-die-with-dignity.

Roberts, Sam. "Census Bureau Gives the Melting Pot a Stir." *New York Times*, August 18, 2008. https://www.nytimes.com/2008/08/18/world/americas/18iht-letter.1.15382517.html.

Rohr, Richard. *The Universal Christ: How a Forgotten Reality Can Change Everything We See, Hope For, and Believe.* New York: Convergent, 2019.

Saad, Lydia. "Catholics' Church Attendance Resumes Downward Slide." https://news.gallup.com/poll/232226/church-attendance-among-catholics-resumes-downward-slide.aspx.

Sanneh, Lamin. *Whose Religion Is Christianity? The Gospel Beyond the West.* Grand Rapids, MI: Eerdmans, 2003.

Seneca. *Epistles 93–124.* Translated by Richard M. Gummere. Cambridge, MA: Harvard University Press, 1925.

Sloan, R. *The Favorable Year of the Lord: A Study of Jubilary Theology in the Gospel of Luke.* Austin, TX: Schola, 1977.

Smith, James K. A. *Imagining the Kingdom: How Worship Works.* Grand Rapids, MI: Baker Academic, 2013.

——— *You Are What You Love: The Spiritual Power of Habit.* Grand Rapids, MI: Brazos, 2016.

Tomberlin, Jim, and Warren Bird. *Better Together: Making Church Mergers Work—Expanded and Updated.* Minneapolis, Minnesota: Fortress, 2020.

Wright, Christopher J. H. *"Here Are Your Gods": Faithful Discipleship in Idolatrous Times.* Downers Grove, IL: InterVarsity, 2020.

——— *The Mission of God: Unlocking the Bible's Grand Narrative.* Downers Grove, IL: InterVarsity, 2006.

Wright, N. T. *The Challenge of Jesus: Rediscovering Who Jesus Was and Is.* Downers Grove, IL: InterVarsity, 2014.

Yonkman, Todd Grant. *Reconstructing Church: Tools for Turning Your Congregation Around.* Lanham, MD: Rowman & Littlefield, 2016.

Made in the USA
Coppell, TX
06 February 2023

12197919R00089